pre**fab**modern

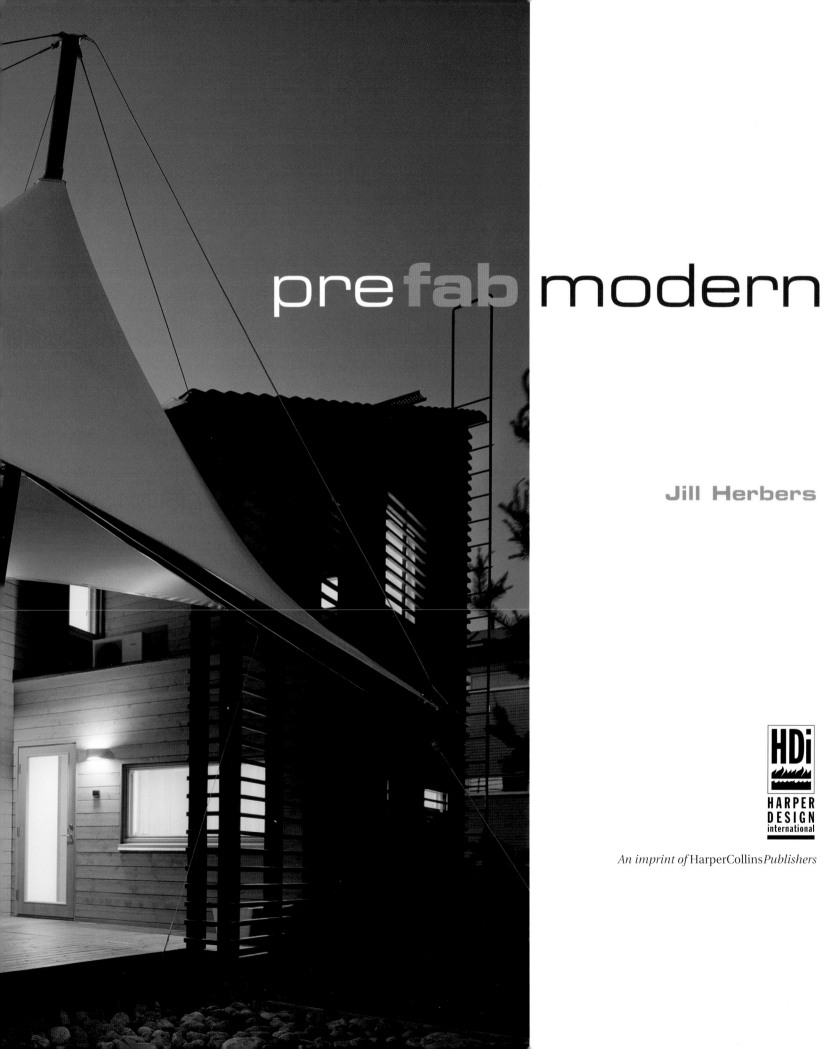

pre**fab** modern

Jill Herbers

HARPER
DESIGN
international

An imprint of HarperCollins*Publishers*

PREFAB MODERN
Copyright © 2004 by
GLITTERATI INCORPORATED
www.GlitteratiIncorporated.com

Text copyright © 2004 by Jill Herbers.

First published in 2004 by
Harper Design International,
An imprint of HarperCollins*Publishers*
10 East 53rd Street
New York, NY 10022
Tel: (212) 207-7000
Fax: (212) 207-7654
HarperDesign@harpercollins.com
www.harpercollins.com

Distributed throughout the world by
HarperCollins International
10 East 53rd Street
New York, NY 10022
Fax: (212) 207-7654

HarperCollins books may be purchased for
educational, business, or sales
promotional use. For information, please
write: Special Markets Department,
HarperCollins*Publishers* Inc., 10 East
53rd Street, New York, NY 10022.

Design: Susi Oberhelman

FIRST EDITION, 2004

Printed and bound in China

1 2 3 4 5 6 7 / 10 09 08 07 06 05 04

Library of Congress
Cataloging-in-Publication Data

Herbers, Jill.
    Prefab modern / Jill Herbers ;
        p. cm.
Includes index.
    ISBN 0-06-058923-X
    1. Prefabricated houses.
    2. Architecture, Domestic.   I. Title.
    NA8480.H47 2004
    690'.81—dc22
                            2003026347

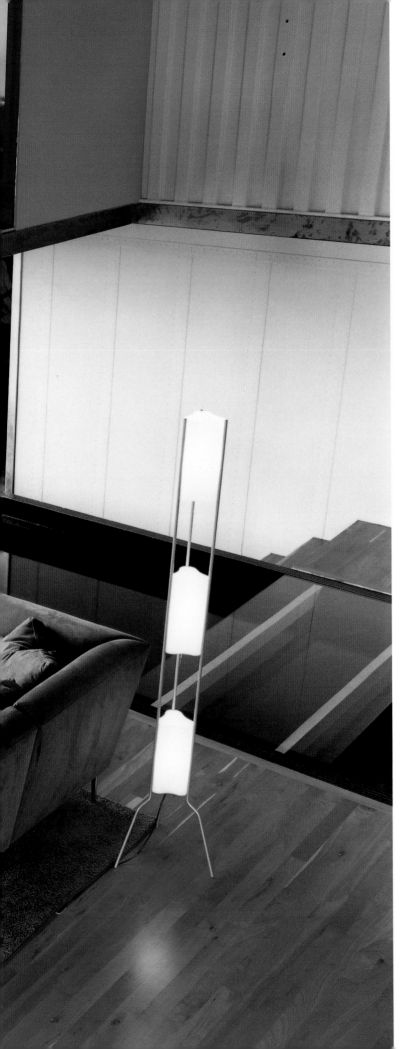

contents

Seatrain House, Los Angeles, 2003, Jennifer Siegal

Introduction

Wallpaper magazine recounted recently the fascinating fact that people who own conventional trailers often wake up with their hair frozen to the wall. The magazine was reporting on a new portable structure that is so beautifully designed it looks like a piece of art sitting on the landscape. It has birch finishes, tongue-and-groove ceilings, and glass-tile mosaic bathrooms; the heating and cooling systems are top grade, and there is a wood-burning stove and wool carpeting, so that nothing will freeze except the ice cream in the high-end refrigerator. To go from trailer trash to trailer chic in one leap is nothing short of revolutionary. Suddenly, prefab has gone from ugly, boxy, or at best, boring, to stylish, smart, and beautiful. What is even more extraordinary is that this portable building and other prefab structures are becoming icons of sorts, sought out for their hipness, high design, and innovation. The fact that they are prefabricated structures, and therefore affordable, sometimes movable, and able to be placed anywhere, just makes it all the better.

A rapidly developing, infinitely exciting movement is happening with prefab today. In addition to aesthetic considerations there is an important sociological element, as well—exceptionally designed houses, with gorgeous materials, can be bought for $100,000 to $200,000. The lowest-priced house in this book is $30,000, including furniture. Another house, built for $50,000, belongs to a violinist with a second-city orchestra that doesn't pay much money and her two-year-old son. Owning a home is part of the American dream, but is has become more and more out of reach for many people. Affordable homes with great design seem miraculous. In many ways, this has been a grassroots movement, with people soliciting architects for prefab homes that are both affordable and beautiful and offer an alternative to the senselessly sprawling houses that have dominated the market. Homeowners are ready to take their house choices into their own hands; they specify prefab to get back to something simpler, something economically feasible—something, if not necessarily portable, that at least can be built for a rational cost on remote sites or in any location where good contractors are hard to find.

Among many examples of how much this movement is influencing the world scene is the fact that Ikea is designing housing in Europe—the BoKlok (which means "smart house") is the latest superstore find. Piercy Connor, a London architect, has created Microflats, a series of prefab apartments that combine efficiency and cutting-edge design. In 2002, a sample apartment was displayed in Selfridges, a London department store window, complete with people living in it for a few days.

The prefab projects in this book include houses that are built with some prefab materials, such as the increasingly popular shipping containers that act as an envelope for design using elements that may not be prefab, as well as houses that are completely made and outfitted in a shop or factory, all the way down to the faucets, and shipped in modules to be put together onsite in a day. There are also projects made from panelized systems, which allow customization and different versions of designs from the same system.

The question of what a house really is has been challenged and enriched by this movement. Here is project after diverse project of imagination and creativity—some of the most wonderful buildings happening in architecture today. ▪

Young Residence, Burleson, Texas, 1997, Richard Wintersole

the **modern** prefab

a brief history

Wherever people have wandered, migration has created a need for cost-effective housing that can be constructed quickly and is also, ideally, portable enough to salvage when it's time to move on. For centuries, tents, caravans, horse-drawn covered wagons, and eventually prefab and mobile homes have served as semipermanent housing solutions. In North America, colonization relied on quick and inexpensive housing—wooden panels for the first prefab house on the continent arrived with colonists in 1624, shipped from England to house a fishing fleet.

The first prefabricated cast-iron house was completed in England in 1830. By the 1840s, foundries in England and America were producing components for metal housing and shipping these semipermanent structure parts to expanding settlements in California, Australia, and Africa. House kits provided temporary housing for miners during the California gold rush of 1849. Precut wooden and panel house kits, as well as many iron buildings, were shipped by mail to house prospectors and the settlements that sprouted up around them.

During the 19th century, the business of making building components that could be assembled on a remote site developed into a substantial industry, known since the 1930s as prefab. Prefabricated struc-

tures would come to include hospitals, schools, warehouses and factories, farm buildings, and railroad stations. Components for prefabricated houses were made first in timber and in corrugated and cast iron, eventually in steel and reinforced concrete. The possibilities of prefab also expanded through the use of new materials such as sheet roofing and linoleum.

At the turn of the 20th century, the existence of these materials as well as improved methods of transportation made it possible for thousands of middle-class Americans to become homeowners by ordering a house from a catalogue. Their ranks swelled by an economic boom, many in the middle class wanted to escape crowded city conditions and move to the greener pastures of suburbia. With housing scarce and new housing labor costs soaring, prefabricated homes offered a relatively inexpensive option. Several companies sold such homes through their catalogues,

including Aladdin, Gordon Van Tine, Montgomery Ward, the Hodgson Company, and Sears, Roebuck and Co. While Sears is today the best known and has sold the most prefab houses, Aladdin was the first, introducing in 1906 their Readi-Cut House, the first true kit house composed of precut, numbered pieces. Altogether, the company sold 65,000 Readi-Cut model homes. They offered 450 models including

OPPOSITE: Ease of construction and affordability were important selling points for early prefab homes as the advertisement from a 1920s Sears, Roebuck and Co., catalogue notes. ABOVE LEFT: The Roseland prefab bungalow created by the Aladdin Company in the 1920s cost $687.80. ABOVE RIGHT: This "compact and convenient" suburban home prefab kit was manufactured by Gordon Van Tine and came with two bedrooms, a living room, dining room, and porch.

instruction book on how to assemble them. Entire homes would arrive by railroad, from precut lumber to carved staircase, down to nails and paint. Sears promotional materials promised that a man "of average abilities" could build the house, and many families worked together to construct a new home. Detailed step-by-step instructions showed buyers how to install a toilet, set up a furnace, and assemble a working sink.

The low cost of mail-order houses even inspired some companies that had also moved to the suburbs to construct entire communities to house their employees. The most expensive neighborhood ever ordered from Sears was Carlinville, Illinois, which was purchased by Standard Oil for the price of one million dollars.

numerous Bungalow types as well as larger Craftsman and Georgian Colonial Revival homes.

Sears, Roebuck and Co., is the name most people associate with mail-order homes. Between 1908 and 1940, Sears sold more than 100,000 mail-order houses, barns, and multiple-family apartment buildings. Homes, ranging from bungalows to mansions, cost from $650 to $2,500. These sturdy, contemporary homes arrived in up to 30,000 pieces, and with a 75-page leather-bound

ABOVE: The Dymaxion House designed in 1927 by Buckminster Fuller—one of only two prototypes constructed in 1947. **OPPOSITE LEFT:** The preserved all-weather aluminum exterior of Dymaxion House. **OPPOSITE RIGHT:** The restored living/dining room with its trademark curved wall of windows and built-in storage units.

Prefab also seemed to offer a solution to the problem of low-cost housing in cities. The need for such housing inspired a New York City–based architect, Grosvenor Atterbury, to develop a construction system based on hollow-cored precast concrete units with story-height wall panels. The components were factory made, transported to the site, and hoisted up by crane. Atterbury built several hundred units in Forest Hills, New York, between 1910 and 1918.

The devastation of World War I and the surplus of steel that followed its end led European architects to prefabricate systems of concrete and steel for housing developments and single-family residences. When first using reinforced concrete in home designs, some builders accurately foresaw that the use of concrete slabs in construction was the method of the future.

In 1914, French architect Le Corbusier, with Max Dubois, designed the Domino House. The design featured a new type of framework made from reinforced concrete that eliminated the need for load-bearing walls. Six columns supported a floating roof and floor slab, while the different floors were linked by cantilevered staircases. Le Corbusier's vision of a new era of mass-produced homes that would do away with "dead concepts in regard to the house" helped to inspire the International Style of architecture, which in turn shaped modern building design throughout the rest of the 20th century and into the 21st. Walter Gropius, founder of the Bauhaus, was also an ardent advocate of mass-produced housing. In 1923, with Adolf Meyer, he developed a "building block" system of standardized

flat-roofed housing and designed a construction system for the Toerten-Dessau housing system.

Examples of the forward-thinking International Style were introduced to the United States in 1932 at the Museum of Modern Art exhibit "The International Style: Architecture Since 1922." Although the exhibit was to influence architects for decades to come, the contents had little immediate effect on the style of mass-produced housing.

"It is difficult to understand what generated this enthusiasm for the concept of the factory-made house, what kept the dream alive," writes Gilbert Herbert in his book, *The Dream of the Factory Made House* (MIT Press, 1984). The challenge of finding a technological solution to the housing crisis was one

obvious spur to much thought and action in the field of prefabrication. For many architects, however, the reward was in the creative and intellectual challenges inherent in the design process rather than with the ultimate realization of the buildings.

One example is the futuristic home design for the Dymaxion House that visionary architect Buckminster Fuller introduced in 1927. The round house was built using tension suspension from a central mast. Fuller's house could easily be disassembled, transported, and reassembled. It had a living/ dining room, two bedrooms, a bathroom, a library, and a sundeck. Fuller's unusual prototype did not meet

with public approval—another exercise of the creative spirit that produced no concrete results.

In 1929, Konrad Wachsmann, one of the leading German exponents of expressionist architecture, built a house for a man known for his creative spirit, a commission that would change the direction of the architect's career. When Wachsmann heard that inventor Albert Einstein wanted to build a summer house in the idyllic town of Caputh, near Potsdam, Germany, he volunteered to build it for him. Wachsmann was so excited at the commission, he quit his day job. To evoke the look of a log cabin, he created a facade of boards running horizontally with a few visible beam ends. The

house's scaffolding consisted of connected beams, while both outer and inner walls and ceiling were built of timber slabs or boards. The roof consisted of tiles. The small house, in which Einstein was surrounded by nature, was lit up by big windows and white window shutters. Before it was erected in Caputh, the house was built on a trial basis at the wood building company Christoph & Unmack AG in Niesky.

Home to many illustrious guests, the house was abandoned when Einstein left Germany in 1933. Because of the Nazis, Einstein never returned to the summer home he described as "paradise," although he did help Wachsmann emigrate to the United States, where the architect would eventually work on postwar prefab housing developments with Walter Gropius. The house still stands, and has recently been made into an insitute in Einstein's honor.

During the 1930s, steel producers continued to sponsor further research into the possibilities of using steel in home construction. This partnership between commerce and design led to notable prefab houses, such as Albert Frey's 1931 Aluminaire House, the first house in America built entirely of light steel and aluminum. Frey, who had worked for and was inspired by Le Corbusier, also borrowed a construction concept from the General Homes Corporation, founded by Howard Fisher in 1932. General Homes modeled its method of constructing homes on the way General Motors produced cars. The construction

company assembled house parts produced by other suppliers, such as General Electric. Frey and fellow designer A. Lawrence Kocher worked with suppliers such as the Aluminum Company of America and a Bethlehem Steel subsidiary to create this contemporary home. Frey would go on to create other prefabricated housing types that made innovative use of aluminum, steel, and canvas.

The collaboration between the steel industry and architects also helped produce a notable steel-framework, steel-decked prototype house that was shown at the Chicago World's Fair of 1933–34. The fair's theme was "A Century of Progress," and one of the attractions that best captured the fair's sense of optimism was the House of Tomorrow. This three-story, 12-sided, glass-walled structure was created by George and William Keck. Shaped like a wedding cake, the house came complete with a hanger to store the family airplane and a machine for cleaning the dishes after every meal, which then probably seemed equally

OPPOSITE LEFT: Following Albert Einstein's request for a "spartan, wooden and practical" summer home, the architect, Konrad Wachsmann, designed the physicist's house to resemble a log cabin. The outer walls were clad with timber slabs punctuated by large windows framed by white shutters. OPPOSITE RIGHT: The living room's wood-paneled interior created a cozy space. Large glass sliding doors let in natural light and provided views of the forest and lake.

fantastical. The house had central heating, air conditioning, and many other then-uncommon amenities. Building it in three days, Keck took the money saved by using prefabricated elements and installed quality-of-life features such as frosted glass in the bathrooms and a built-in aquarium in the children's room. Thousands of fair goers flocked to see the house, paying 10 cents admission, but for most homeowners, the design was too futuristic. It was also, at that time, difficult to get a loan on any kind of design that was modern.

As the Great Depression took its toll on the housing industry, more American companies began to experiment with prefab in order to produce affordable housing. Robert McLaughlin of American Homes introduced a brand known as American Motohomes—simple two-story, flat-roofed houses inspired by the International Style—but the sparely designed homes did not elicit an enthusiastic response from buyers.

Frank Lloyd Wright saw the idea of creating an affordable house as a design challenge and tackled it

with his usual maverick flair. "The house of moderate cost is not only America's major architectural problem but the problem most difficult for her major architects," he said. To solve this problem, he conceived what he called the Usonian house. His elegant creation was built with a grid system for maximum flexibility. Costs were cut by repeating standard details and eliminating such features as a visible roof, gutters, basement, and garage. Other deletions included radiators, light fixtures, paint, and plaster. Wright designed two dozen Usonian houses in the mid-1930s and 1940s. In 1959, he would build the first of his series of prefab houses for a Wisconsin builder named Marshall Erdman. Prefab No. 1, as it was known, featured built-in cabinetry and mahogany-paneled walls. Wright provided every detail, including a grand piano and a mailbox. The house still stands today on Staten Island, the only existing Wright design in New York City besides the Guggenheim Museum.

World War II created such a dramatic housing shortage that the U.S. government was compelled to develop and support prefab housing, first to house troops during the war and then, after the war, to house returning GIs. As American involvement in the war loomed, the Navy knew it would face a huge logistical problem moving and housing troops. To create a workable solution, it contacted the George A. Fuller construction company in New York to design an improved Nissen hut, a lightweight structure developed by the British during World War I. Designers

OPPOSITE ABOVE: A view of the House of Tomorrow from the roof deck towards the house. Built by George and William Keck, the prefab home came complete with central air conditioning and a dishwasher. It was considered a model of futuristic living at the 1933–34 Chicago World's Fair. OPPOSITE BELOW: First-floor living room with large glass windows and historic chairs original to the house. OPPOSITE RIGHT: View of spiral staircase leading to the turret.

Peter DeJongh and Otto Brandenberger set up a production center near Quonset, Rhode Island.

The design of the Quonset hut, which inherited its name from the location of its production plant, may have been inspired by Iroquois lodges. The skeleton of these lightweight portable huts was a row of semicircular steel ribs covered with corrugated sheet metal. The ribs sat on a low steel-frame foundation and had a plywood floor. The standard huts were 20 feet wide and 48 feet long with 720 square feet of floor space. A larger model measured 40 by 100 feet. The arched form was strong and lightweight. Improvements over the Nissen hut included a pressed wooden lining, insulation, and a tongue-and-groove wooden floor.

About 170,000 Quonset huts were produced during the war and many survive today, adapted into industrial buildings, churches, and stores. Many returning veterans occupied Quonset huts by choice. Universities made them into student housing. Architects took interest in them and adapted these durable icons. Two of the most innovative uses for Quonset huts are the home and studio designed for painter Robert Motherwell, and architect Bruce Goff's modernist Quonset chapel in Camp Parks, California.

After the war, the urgent need for housing kept the government in the prefabrication business. Many munitions factories were converted into prefab manufacturing plants as part of a federally subsidized housing boom. Public funds financed the production

of 200,000 units built by nearly 70 companies. Several of these designs were modular and used metal parts. Three companies in the prefab industry received direct federal loans, of which two produced steel houses— General Panel Corporation and the Lustron Corporation. General Panel Corporation houses were designed by Walter Gropius and Konrad Wachsmann, who had

OPPOSITE LEFT: Living room of Frank Lloyd Wright's Usonian Exhibition House, Guggenheim Museum, New York. OPPOSITE ABOVE: Usonian exterior with Wright's trademark corner and ribbon windows. OPPOSITE BELOW: With space at a premium, the interior of Wright's compact prefab came with recessed bookshelves and cabinets. ABOVE: Exterior of Quonset hut residence, Hawaii, 1950.

both emigrated from Germany during the war. The houses used interchangeable parts and a standardized system. New building materials such as enamel and aluminum were used to make construction less expensive and time consuming. However, fewer than two hundred of General Panel's well-conceived and carefully engineered Package Houses were produced before the company went out of business in 1951. General Panel's failure was a major blow to the prefab movement, many believing that if the contributions of Gropius and Wachsmann could not realize the dream of creating factory-built houses, no one's could.

The Lustron Corporation also began producing prefabricated all-steel houses in 1948 in a former aircraft factory. Although these buildings were rightfully described as the houses "America was talking about," the company encountered insurmountable production problems and faced bankruptcy by 1950. Lustron had received 20,000 orders by 1948 but most of them remained unfilled. Problems, such as parts that were not truly interchangeable and that were difficult to transport, limited the company's delivery to fewer than two thousand houses.

OPPOSITE: Exterior of a fully restored Lustron home from 1950 with its signature enameled sheet metal panels making painting unnecessary. The exterior could be cleaned by simply hosing down walls.

Reasoning that a designer's touch might help make prefab housing more palatable, in 1950 the French government commissioned furniture designer Jean Prouvé to devise a plan for aesthetically pleasing mass-produced housing. Prouvé wanted to avoid the repetitiveness and often drab monotony associated with prefab housing, so he developed a plan that featured 14 variations of two design types. "Raw materials and methods of shaping them vary," said Prouvé. "The creative minds who choose them and match them and very often see them through to completion are equally diverse."

Twenty-five units were built according to Prouvé's design and installed in a pilot program in Meudon, France. They were produced very quickly, each delivered by a single truck and assembled in a single day by a four-man team. The light, dynamic houses were designed to be built without scaffolding. Composed of steel, aluminum, and timber, the thermally insulated Meudon homes were designed for large-scale production. While all the original houses were sold, the French government chose not to adopt the design for low-cost housing and no more of Prouvé's homes were produced.

Around the same time, devloper William Levitt was using prefabricated structures to set the standard for the postwar American suburb. Capitalizing on the housing crunch of the postwar years, Levitt built communities. He offered small, detached single-family houses to the 12 million returning GIs who were coming home to live in attics, basements, and Quonset huts. In 1947, he started building rental homes, and by 1948, he was putting up 150 homes a week, bringing workers to the site to pour foundations, erect frames, and install plumbing. The more houses built, reasoned Levitt, the lower the cost. His housing developments would successfully transform the building industry from a custom enterprise into an assembly-line industry and create a template for American life. While the idea of large-scale suburban housing developments had been talked about since the 1930s, no one else had successfully realized it, before or since.

Levitt's most famous development—and one that continues to bear his name—is Levittown, New York, where he built a community of spartan, look-alike boxes on potato fields. Levittown is perhaps the most idealized and yet also the most criticized development in planned housing. For many families, these prefab homes were a chance to escape crowded living arrangements. Advertisements boasted of a front window from the kitchen, so the housewife could watch the kids while cooking, plus a Bendix washer, General Electric refrigerator, and stainless steel cabinets to make her housework easier. The typical Levittown home in 1950 had a foyer, a living room with a fireplace, two bedrooms, a bath, and a kitchen, plus a porch or carport. Aluminum blinds covered the windows. Glass was insulated and TV sets were

built in. The cookie-cutter homes clustered along winding drives off of parkways leading to the city, from which many of their occupants had moved. There was some variation in style—the Lookout Cape, the Snug Harbor Cape, the Green Hills, the Mariner—but the homes were still criticized for their uniformity, cramped interiors, and bleak landscap-

ing. As time passed and families grew, the small houses sprouted dormers, garages, breezeways, and wings. As incomes grew, many of the homes had makeovers. Today, it is hard to find two that are alike.

Another postwar influence on today's home construction is the Case Study Houses program. It was launched by John Entenza, then editor of *Arts*

and Architecture magazine. Between 1945 and 1962, 36 Case Study houses would be designed by architects such as Richard Neutra, Pierre Koenig, and Charles and Ray Eames, taking many of them from obscurity to international fame.

Under the program, each house was intended to be a case study of the needs of a particular client, each representing a different type of homeowner. In the case study designed by Charles and Ray Eames, the house was designed for them, using themselves as an example of a working couple with no children and needing space for both work and domestic life. The house was completely built of prefabricated parts, many of them steel. "It was the idea of using materials in a different way, materials that could be bought from a catalog," said Ray Eames, "so that there was a continuation of the idea of mass production, so that people would not have to build stick by stick, but with material that comes ready-made off the shelf." The Eames Case Study consisted of twin buildings, constructed proudly of factory materials and tucked into a hillside behind a row of trees. One housed living space, the other work space. Construction took a few months with the frame being raised in a day and a half. The house used ample expanses of glass to invite nature in.

Pierre Koenig's prefab house, an elegant minimalist glass block, captures the "brave new world" spirit of late-20th-century architecture and sums up everything that seems glamorous about the 1960s.

Hovering almost weightlessly above Los Angeles, it has been described as a giant Rubik's cube and as "James Bond meets Holly Golightly in Hollywood." Because the house was built on a small lot, Koenig used a steel frame squared with the lot lines, then placed another steel frame inside that was twisted 30 degrees toward the desired view. This helped create the slightly dangerous feeling of hanging over a cliff, although the house was probably more earthquake-safe than its neighbors.

Craig Ellwood's Case Study houses demonstrated that architecture could be both elegantly simple and financially attainable. The clarity and simplicity of his techniques are seen in all his Case Study houses. In the Johnson House (1952–53), he used an easy-to-assemble steel and timber structural system in a frame construction that suited the hillside site. In the Hale House (1949–51), he created an uninterrupted recessed glass facade and reduced the roof to a thin wafer, with 10-inch timber roof beams. At the Rosen House (1961–63), he used masonry panels to fill

OPPOSITE LEFT: Charles Eames's design for the exterior of the Eames Case Study House used a variety of prefabricated components in an inventive way. Sheets of glass were juxtaposed with stucco panels painted in white and primary colors, which were framed by steel grids. OPPOSITE RIGHT: The two-story-high living room used large plates of glass for windows and sliding doors to invite nature in.

ABOVE: Pierre Koenig's intersecting planes of steel and glass in his design for Case Study House #21 (1956–58) combined high design with low-cost materials to create affordable and livable homes. Koenig's basic design solutions for prefab housing have stood the test of time and can be seen in many contemporary prefab designs.

in the crisp steel framing and repeated an open-box section detail along the steel entablature on either side of the house. "The spirit of architecture is its truthfulness to itself—its clarity and logic with respect to its materials and structure," said Ellwood.

Another trend that helped shape housing in the 1950s was mobile homes. Some of the earliest examples of mobile homes were the horse-drawn ones built by roaming bands of European Gypsies in the 1500s. America's first mobile homes, beach properties that could be moved by teams of horses on the outer banks of North Carolina, were built in the 1870s.

Mobile homes as they are known today began in 1926, with trailers pulled by cars, known as trailer coaches. Excited by their new ability to travel across country in cars, Americans wanted to take extended road trips and take their homes with them. By 1943, trailers averaged a width of eight feet and were over 20 feet in length, usually having as many as four bedrooms but no bathrooms. By 1948, lengths reached 30 feet and bathrooms were added. Mobile homes continued to grow in every dimension, and by 1954, Marshfield Homes had created Ten-Wide, a mobile home exactly that many feet in width. While most mobile homes continued to look like trailers, a high-end few tried to capture the avant-garde look of industrial design. In the 1950s and 1960s, mobile homes would be developed that mimicked the designs of such notable architects as Frank Lloyd Wright and Mies van der Rohe.

In the 1930s, some designers predicted that the age of the mobile home was at hand. Although their tawdry reputation as temporary shelter and their limited space kept mobile homes from becoming the standard for housing, by the 1960s homes on wheels would account for 15 percent of all the money spent on habitats in the United States. By 1968, they

ABOVE: Hale House, designed by Craig Ellwood, was completed in 1951. For many Case Study House architects, sensitivity to one's surroundings was as important as using affordable industrial materials. Ellwood's slim, unobtrusive beams appear to effortlessly lift the structure off the ground. The recessed slabs of the facade form the perfect foil for the adjacent trees.

ABOVE: A school in Jamaica made from shipping containers provided by Global Peace Containers, a nonprofit organization. Shipping containers can withstand extreme weather conditions such as tornadoes and hurricanes, making them ideal sustainable housing. OPPOSITE: Buckminster Fuller's geodesic dome designed for the American pavilion at the World Expo in Montreal in 1967 was a spectacular structure. This large-scale prefab was created from thousands of Plexiglas triangular panels held together by stainless steel components. The dome stood 20 stories high at two hundred feet and spanned 250 feet in diameter with no internal support structure.

would account for 25 percent of all single-family homes. In 1976, the U.S. Congress passed the National Manufactured Housing Construction and Safety Act to ensure that homes were built according to approved standards. In 1980, Congress approved changing the name of mobile homes to "manufactured homes."

That legislation was prompted by the substandard quality of many prefab and manufactured homes built in the postwar years. As a result, the industry looked for ways to improve prefabrication quality and overhaul its image. For example, a company named Techbuilt designed a prefab housing system of converging components that could be used at the builder's and owner's discretion. This repackaging of the concept helped the company achieve success in the 1950s and 1960s. Judging that prefab's lack of appeal to the general public was due to its industrial look, some companies began producing wholly or partially built houses in styles such as Colonial or Cape Cod.

Other designers continued to experiment with new shapes, mediums, and materials, even if there was no immediate practical or market application. After designing lightweight homes and streamlined cars, in 1954 Buckminster Fuller had patented the icosahedron, a 20-sided polyhedron with each side made up of an equilateral triangle. By the 1960s, he was building structures based on the icosahedron, a breakthrough in building technology he called the geodesic dome. The geodesic dome combines the sphere, the most efficient container of volume per square foot, with the tetrahedron, which provides the greatest strength for the least volume of weight. A properly constructed dome can withstand winds of 210 miles per hour, while at the same time is light and easily transportable. Though they can be put up in hours, geodesic domes have withstood earthquakes and hurricanes better than conventional buildings. In 1967, the U.S. Information Agency commissioned Fuller to design the American Pavilion at the World Expo in Montreal. The Expo Dome he created was a geodesic three-quarter sphere. Since then, 200,000 geodesic domes have been built and used for homes and shelters.

The latest frontier for prefab has been homes made from shipping containers, often used for both temporary and permanent structures that easily withstand hurricanes, tornadoes, and earthquakes. Their low cost, strength, and ease and speed with which they can be used make them ideal prefab housing for third-world countries in need of immediate housing. For example, Global Peace Containers, a U.S.–based nonprofit organization, has perfected a method of converting retired shipping containers into sustainable housing and community buildings, such as schools. Since they are designed to withstand heavy loads, they are versatile, supporting a second floor, for instance, and can be assembled in a variety of configurations.

However prefab develops in the future, it will remain a collaboration between aesthetic and technological creativity, sometimes pragmatic, sometimes merely a horizon-expanding ideal. ▪

CHAPTER 2

the profiles

richard **wintersole**

ABOVE: The elegance of the house is in its simplicity. RIGHT: The steel frame for the house cost $17,000 and was put up in just a few days. The exterior finish is made of stucco and Galvalume siding.

"We're on the forefront of the residential revolution," says Mike Young of the house that he and his wife, Gayla LaBry, had built by architect Richard Wintersole in Burleson, Texas, a suburb of Fort Worth. The movement toward prefab is indeed nothing short of revolutionary, potentially changing the way houses are chosen, bought, and made, and affecting everything from who can afford them to how they look. The idea that prefab is more than a trend and is actually becoming a movement has huge implications. If people can buy good design at a price they can afford, or buy a house by clicking on their computer, or customize their own house within design systems so they are practically designing it themselves, the revolution is economic, sociological, and aesthetic. In the case of this house, the appearance alone is enough to alert one to the fact that something new is going on. As Young says, "It doesn't look like anything else around."

In 1997, Young and LaBry were looking for a prefab house on the Internet for their half-acre lot and couldn't find anything that was both well designed and affordable. "I only saw cheap details, and poor layouts with no rhyme or reason," says Young. After he saw a steel frame used in an addition at the warehouse where he works as an industrial engineer, he

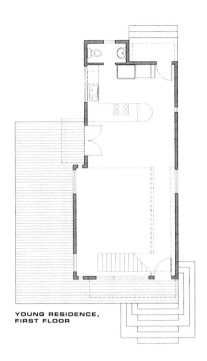

YOUNG RESIDENCE,
SECOND FLOOR

YOUNG RESIDENCE,
FIRST FLOOR

got the idea to use a steel frame for their home and have the inside designed for them. The couple commissioned Wintersole, who went to Classic Steel Homes in Houston with custom drawings, which they agreed to produce in a quite remarkable joining of industrial-age materials and IT-era processes: "They feed the design into a computer and it then directs how to bend the metal, shape it and cut it," Wintersole explains.

The red iron frame, metal studs, beams, roof, siding, even the screws—"everything that was steel," says Wintersole—came on a truck from the company. The pieces were placed in the yard, "like big Tinkertoys," according to Wintersole, and assembled like an Ikea desk. "They bolted it together and boom!

It was done," says Young. It took just a few days and $17,000 for the frame to be completed.

The metal structure had a lot of unexpected advantages beyond the convenience of quick assembly. This may be the only house in "Tornado Alley" that can easily stand up to 80-mile-per-hour winds.

LEFT: Basic materials were used for both aesthetics and budget. To play off of the steel structure, the stairs are diamond-plate steel and the railings are sandblasted steel. ABOVE: A double-height living room creates a loftlike space. The floors on the second story are sealed plywood.

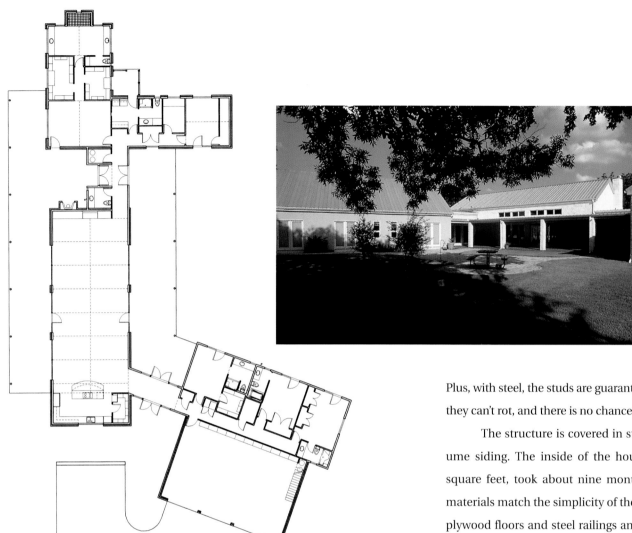

GARRETT RESIDENCE: FIRST FLOOR

ABOVE and **RIGHT**: One of the reasons that today's prefab is successful is that it is remarkably diverse and goes beyond all kinds of stereotypes. The Garrett residence in Hood County, Texas, proves that a rambling ranch house can benefit from a prefab steel structure just as much as the more compact houses that are on the market. Stucco and limestone form the exterior.

Plus, with steel, the studs are guaranteed to be straight, they can't rot, and there is no chance of termites.

The structure is covered in stucco and Galvalume siding. The inside of the house, which is 950 square feet, took about nine months to finish. The materials match the simplicity of the steel frame, with plywood floors and steel railings and stairs. The total cost of the house was about $120,000.

Wintersole maintains that the same system can create many different kinds of houses and designs, in "small, medium, and large," he says. "It doesn't have to look like an airstreamed trailer," he notes, talking about the use of metal and prefab. His house for Jenks and Denise Garrett in Hood County, Texas, couldn't be any different from the Youngs', but a prefab steel frame is also its central element. A 7,000-square-foot ranch covered in stucco and limestone, it has three wings—a master suite, an office wing, and

what the Garretts call a "motel wing" for guests. In this house, the skeleton of the metal beams show beautifully, crisscrossing everywhere above the long living, dining, and kitchen areas. This sense of being in a barn structure but with metal inside has led the Garretts to refer to their home as "redneck contemporary."

To use such an industrial material and still capture the essence of a region is a perfect example of how prefab can adapt to different areas of the country, styles, and personal needs and tastes. With the metal roof, Wintersole has managed to honor the agricultural architecture that is so important to the vernacular of Texas, recalling metal-roofed chicken coops, for example. Then details build on the regional references: In the kitchen, Wintersole had cabinets made from native pecan trees—the same kind that the couple see by the hundred when they look outside.

A similarly personal touch was also applied in the Young house, where Wintersole, acknowledging the couple's Louisiana roots and the tradition of raised houses to avoid floods, raised the house nine inches on a pier-and-beam foundation to give them a better view, provide for a wood deck, and limit contact with the soil for environmental reasons. Wintersole's work is a stunning testament to the fact that it is what you do with prefab that makes all the difference, that something as seemingly impersonal as a steel box can be made into the most individual of homes, at the same time celebrating the steel in all its power and aesthetic distinction. ■

LEFT: The steel beams are exposed. "Being able to see the steel or any other building material," says Wintersole, "you're telling the story of how the house was built." ABOVE: There is a very finished, elegant look to the house, at the same time that the steel plays a major role in defining it.

heikkinen–komonen **architects**

It could be argued that the most chic, interesting, and innovative architectural designs today are pre-fab. It has been generally acknowledged for a while now that there has been something of a vacuum in architectural design, along with the rest of the arts. As the search continues for what is really original and exciting and new, so much has been recycled and so much is shallow that it doesn't qualify for serious consideration as to what architecture is or can be today. Because prefab is what is happening now and because its designs often come from need—considerations about cost and site and construction—it is producing the really interesting houses. It is from limitations that creativity often arises, and from the grass roots—people who are looking for ways to make housing work for them.

One look at the "Touch" house and it is obvious that this is one of those buildings, one that stands out as a fresh, striking structure that projects something new in its design and aesthetic. Created by Finnish architects Mikko Heikkinen and Markku Komonen, it is arresting and hip. This is what Heikkinen–Komonen intended. An astonishing 90 percent of houses in Finland are prefab, but they are everything from traditional to boring to unattractive.

The architects wanted to offer a modern house for younger families that would fit into both urban and suburban neighborhoods.

The house is designed to accommodate four people, and with 2,078 square feet it is comfortably roomy, but not in the way one might expect because the space is laid out uniquely. "The house has a simple, contained character from the outside, but inside is spatially rich and full of light," says Heikkinen. Beyond the slatted exterior, a contemporary form of lattice, are several outdoor spaces. All of these areas sit beneath the pitched roof and within the slatting, so they are part of the house while remaining outdoors. The spaces include a veranda, a balcony off the master bedroom, and a sauna terrace. The tiled roof has glass portions above each space to further the outdoor ambience and to let light into the rest

LEFT: The house has a unique form of slatting that contains outdoor rooms on two sides that are two stories high. The areas include a veranda, a balcony off the master bedroom, and a sauna terrace. Above them, the tile ceiling that covers the rest of the house changes to glass so light can come in and make the space more like the outdoors.

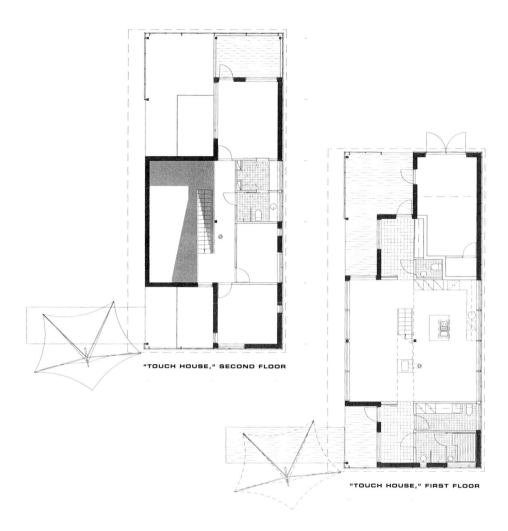

"TOUCH HOUSE," SECOND FLOOR

"TOUCH HOUSE," FIRST FLOOR

of the house. It is a new take on how to integrate exterior and interior.

Within, the rooms are grouped around a general area that Komonen calls a "farmhouse" living space. This includes the living room, dining area, and kitchen. It is likened to a farmhouse because of the one-and-a-half-story space and because of the general mood of traditional domesticity, though

ABOVE: The slatted areas show the placement of the outdoor rooms. RIGHT: Slatting of a different size on the picture window echoes the exterior of the house, while the window brings in even more light. The sail canopy was added as an additional detail by the owners.

within there is a very contemporary aesthetic. This space centers around the wood-burning stove, which Heikkinen–Komonen compare to the kitchen stove as the "heart" of the home in traditional structures. Areas for living, dining, and cooking are of different heights, and are distinguished by their furnishings.

The wood exterior of the home is made from large prefabricated units that are assembled at a factory. The surfaces are finished at the factory, as well, but the rest of the finishes were done with regular construction methods. It is a strikingly sleek and refined interior, with simple and elegant finishes. The slatting that runs outside the house creates a design element that can be seen from the windows all around, creating a visual continuity. The overall effect is a serene, unusually artistic house. The detail of the entire structure is so intricate and of such high craftsmanship that it is enough to blow away the old reputation of "cardboard box" prefab housing forever.

The lesson about prefab here is that an architecture firm doesn't have to specialize in prefab houses in order to make a successful one. Heikkinen–Komonen just knows how to meet challenges creatively. They designed a headquarters building for McDonald's in Helsinki that is a chic cylindrical structure, and a villa made from stabilized earth in Guinea. In the case of the "Touch" house, the architecture firm was commissioned to design the prototype by a building company, Kannustalo Ltd. The house was then exhibited at the Tuusula Housing

LEFT and ABOVE: Looking at these pictures of the interior of the house anywhere outside this book, one would never guess it is a prefab structure. The materials and the detailing of the dining area, kitchen, and living space are of higher quality than most "stick-built" homes today. Part of this has to do with the European aesthetic reflected by the architects.

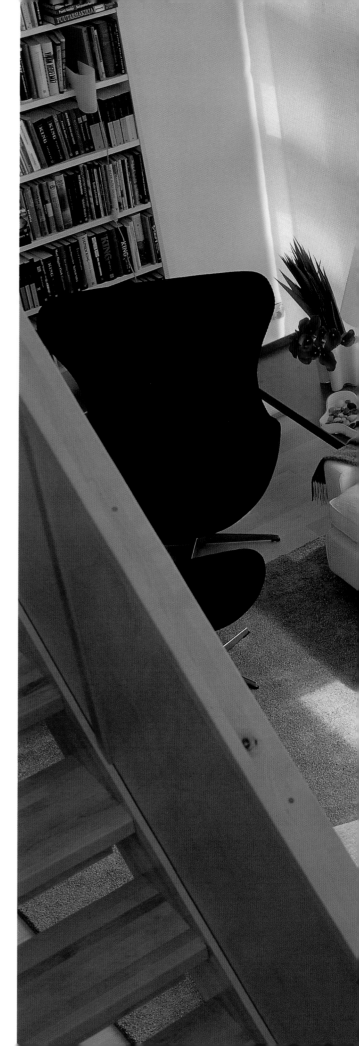

Fair in Finland in 2000, where it was enthusiastically received. The house has now been made for homeowners around the world, from New York to New Zealand to Korea. The Kannustalo factory can now produce upwards of 10 houses a year.

It seems to be working to keep up with orders, but since this house has barely been published, it is still possible to get in line for one. ▪

ABOVE and RIGHT: The master bedroom sits on the second floor, above the one-and-a-half-story living area. The living room flows into the dining and kitchen spaces, making the house open. The extensive amount of light that comes in through the picture window enhances that feeling.

adam **kalkin**

Architect Adam Kalkin's own house in Bernardsville, New Jersey, is a testament to how personal prefab can be. Though the house is made primarily of transoceanic shipping containers, a steel shell, aluminum garage doors, and cinder blocks to form interior rooms, it is more precisely individual than most homes anywhere, of any kind—so much so that it still surprises Kalkin and his family. It is also proof that there is no one way to think about prefab and that no one can ever own the idea of it—prefab is as many different concepts as there are architects who work with it and homeowners who live in the designs they create. In Kalkin's case, it is using these almost alarmingly basic prefab materials to create a limitless number of designs for the shell of the house and then pretty much suggesting that the shell matters only as much as what you do with it, and what you do within it. Because of their simplicity, these houses are envelopes for ideas.

In his own steel-and-shipping-container home, Kalkin has a cottage from the 1800s that was already on the land and inhabited by the gardener who tended it. He enclosed it with this new 33-foot-high shell of a home. The clapboard cottage has been kept as a domestic space, with the porch retained as a dining area, and the inside holding the kitchen, a library, and a guest room with a second-story balcony that overlooks the interior of the house. By putting a house within a house, particularly a historic one within an industrial-style one, the idea of what a house is gets raised and explored. Why the two work together remains something of a mystery, although Kalkin does mention that he "loves the maritime romance of the shipping containers" and the romance of a gardener's cottage is a given. Designer Albert Hadley, who is a living symbol of traditionalism from his work with Sister Parish, did the decoration for the home. This is not anyone's expectation of prefab, and yet here it is: intensely personal, intimately domestic, and from many vistas, very formal.

On the other side of the cottage is a group of rooms made of cinder block that form the bed and

LEFT: Kalkin's residence is a celebration of the shipping container as house exterior—almost the entire container is used with little structural modification. He has followed the lead of Buckminster Fuller, who made living spaces out of steel grain silos for troops during World War II.

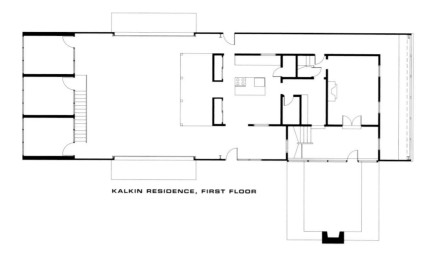

KALKIN RESIDENCE, FIRST FLOOR

ABOVE TOP and BOTTOM: The cottage contains the traditionally domestic spaces of the house, with the dining room on its porch, the kitchen just inside the front door, and the formal living room sitting within it. RIGHT: Within the container is a cottage dating from the 1800s.

bath areas of the house. Here, the walls are glass (with curtains for privacy) and the floors on the stair landings are leather. A living area separates the cottage and the cinder-block rooms. Kalkin compares this space to a plaza, with a view of the little house on one side and the complex of rooms looking like a city building on the other.

Light could probably be considered one of the design materials of this house, one that is completely prefab and already existing at the site. The exterior walls on either side of the house are glass grids covering the entire surface, and on a third side of the house, the windows are cut in the shape of a gable roof to echo and honor that of the cottage that sits

just within. Fourteen-foot garage doors on two sides of the house open to let the outside in—the curtain for one of the doors has a cross shape cut into it so that when it is down and the sun shines in, there is a distinctive design of light on the floor.

LEFT: Standard garage doors open to the center of the house, where a living area resembles a plaza, as it is in the middle of several spaces. ABOVE, LEFT and RIGHT: About designing the interior, Albert Hadley says, "I brought a certain element of civilization to something that is, let's face it, over-the-top—literally. Strangely enough, I think it's all come together."

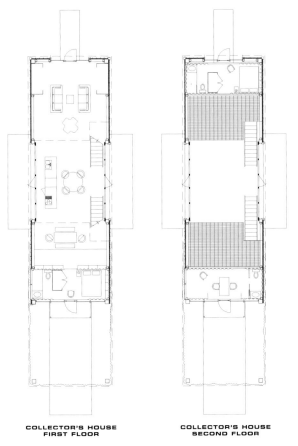

ABOVE, LEFT and RIGHT: The Collector's House at the Shelburne Museum in Shelburne, Vermont, was also made from shipping containers and has an interior designed by Albert Hadley, who showcased the museum's folk art in the house. The space has an open design, and though it is a theoretical house, it is a triumphant design that conveys a sense of home.

Kalkin has taken the same basic elements of steel, glass, shipping containers, and garage doors and designed other stunning spaces that contain different, equally striking ideas. The Collector's House, a piece for the public at the Shelburne Museum in Vermont that features shipping containers painted orange and green for interior walls and that was also decorated by Albert Hadley, shows off antiques and other collections of the museum in complete elegance.

His 99K House, so named for its price of $99,000, uses the same materials and features a central set of stairs that is a focal point due to its intricate balconies and interesting multitude of stairs and rails. Kalkin gets right into the spirit of prefab in his presentation of the house, where he writes, matter-of-factly, "Buy this house by calling 908-696-1987."

Kalkin has also created "The Butler Variations," a catalogue of designs that use Butler steel shells to compose what Kalkin calls Seven Utopian Houses. As if ordering from a Land's End catalogue, the consumer opens it up to find that the 20-Foot Triple Stack is comprised of a 33-by-40-foot Butler building, three 20-foot Trans-Oceanic shipping containers, and two aluminum garage doors, and costs $79,000. The 40-Foot Triple Stack is $150,000, the Hybrid House is $185,000, and the House for Anne and Matt, now available to anyone, is $250,000.

Kalkin says he uses materials that differ from those used in standard homes because they work. He describes them as "opportunistic" in many ways because they make sense and are inexpensive. "I like these buildings because you don't have to design them. You just cut them up and do what you want with them."

The materials are so basic, in fact, that Kalkin's very latest design is a house that can be assembled by the owner, like the balsawood model airplanes that were sold in dime stores. Called the Quik Build House, it is now available for about $50,000. Made of the same steel-shell material as many of his other designs, it is the essence of simplicity, but with an elegance that makes it worthy of this new breed of prefab homes. ■

ABOVE: The Collector's House succeeds because of the coming together of opposites. The sleek metal of the shipping containers is a perfect contrast to the handmade folk art that the building was created to hold. Of course, it is in the hands of these two "artists," Kalkin and Hadley, that it works. The inherent beauty of the containers also is allowed to shine in this context.

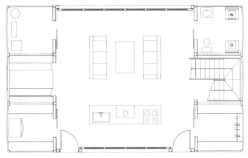

QUIK BUILD HOUSE, FIRST FLOOR

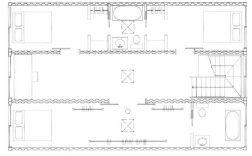

QUIK BUILD HOUSE, SECOND FLOOR

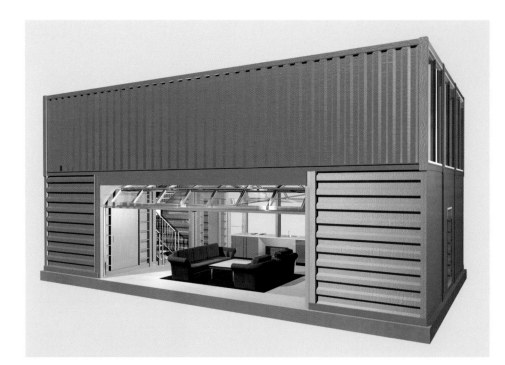

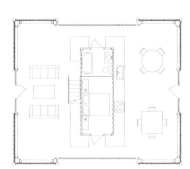

99K HOUSE, FIRST FLOOR

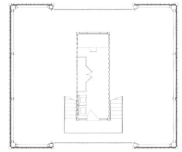

99K HOUSE, SECOND FLOOR

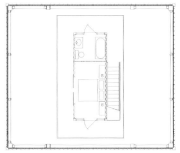

99K HOUSE, THIRD FLOOR

TOP, LEFT and RIGHT: The Quik Build House is perfect as a second home, with guests perhaps helping in the assembly. "You can do it yourself with a forklift," says Kalkin, "or get a team to build it." ABOVE and NEAR RIGHT: The 99K House, on sale for $99,000, is spacious for its price, with three stories constructed from shipping containers. FAR RIGHT: These are four of Kalkin's designs for Seven Utopian Houses, a variation of plans made from Butler steel shells, garage doors, and containers.

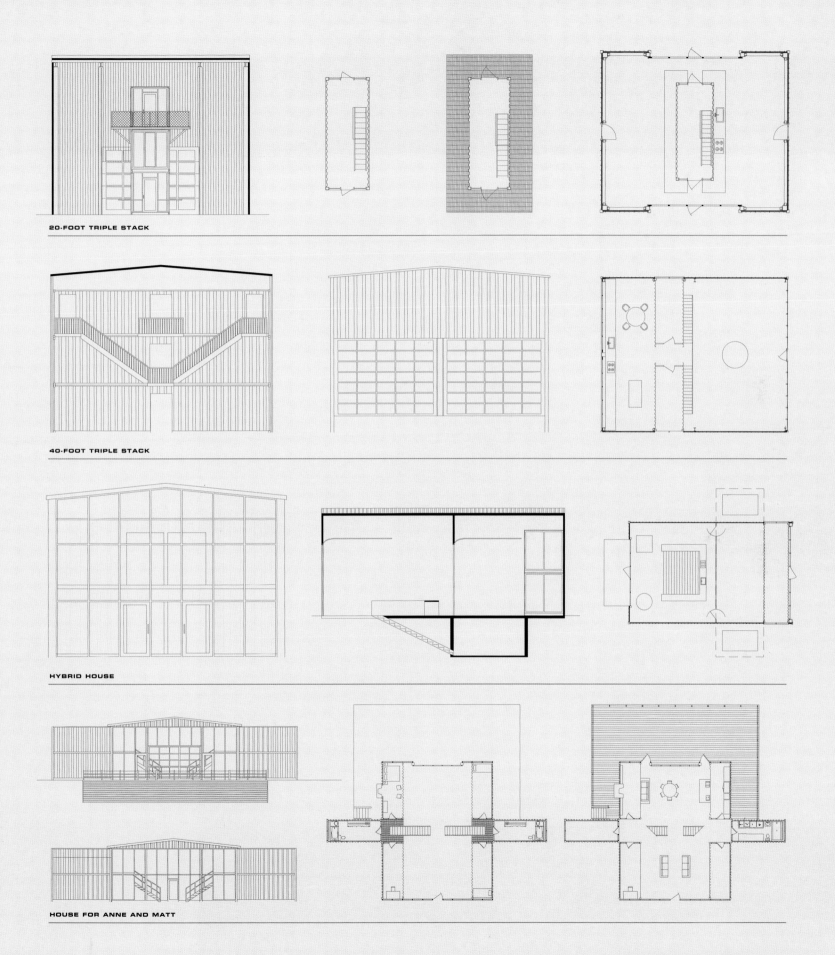

20-FOOT TRIPLE STACK

40-FOOT TRIPLE STACK

HYBRID HOUSE

HOUSE FOR ANNE AND MATT

rocio **romero**

Many of today's prefab houses have a distinctive presence on the landscape or streetscape—using copius amounts of glass, they look like houses of light. Indeed they *are* houses of light. To see Rocio Romero's LV Home glowing at night or lit up during the day when the sun comes in is to witness a work of light as well as architecture, the house resembles a giant version of one of those light-based artworks that can be seen in contemporary art museums. Romero had this luminous effect in mind when she created the LV Home, a house for her mother in Laguna Verde (hence "LV") on the Pacific Coast of Chile. "It was so clear for me that this vacation home had to be all about having the exterior become the interior landscape," she says, and a big part of the exterior in Chile is sun.

The house has sliding doors all along one side and a window wall at the end, making a view into the landscape part of the interior. Designing the 970-square-foot house so that it stretches out long and with nine-foot ceilings allows it to take in even more

LEFT: The LV Home is a complete kit house that can be had for about $75,000 to $120,000. Among the reasons for the low cost is that the one-time design and engineering fees are included in the price, the parts are inexpensive because of lower labor prices, and the plans reduce time for the contractor.

of the outside. Romero wanted to create a house that was relaxed but refined, something that was low-maintenence but that was aesthetically worthy of the gorgeous surroundings, which consists of forested land that comes down to the sea in a stunning slope.

ABOVE and **RIGHT**: The house can be ordered online, somewhat miraclously, from the architect or from livemodern.com. The layout is simple but brilliant because it fits two bedrooms into a relatively small space and because the rooms that are most lived-in are in the front, where the views and light are, and the less-used spaces, like the entry, are in the back.

It also had to be inexpensive. "My mom didn't want to spend more than $30,000, and that was that," she says. American labor makes that figure much higher, and Romero and her mother also saved money by acting as general contractors.

The simplicity of the design as well as the materials, which consist mostly of glass, metal, and some wood for the frame, helped bring the cost down and made it easy to put together. The floor plan is extremely smart and simple. The main living areas and the two bedrooms run along the glass front of the house to take advantage of the view and the bathrooms, kitchen, and laundry room were put in the back. "I was interested in developing a prototype for a mass-producible home,"

says Romero, "so simple, straightforward gestures as well as dimensions that made it easy for the house to be trucked to the site were the constraints I imposed on the home." Romero came back to St. Louis, where she lives, and put the house into production. A factory about an hour outside the city is making the house, and it is ready to order by website.

For $29,195 plus shipping costs, the shell of the house will be shipped along with plans and instructions for the contractors, a list of to-dos, a construction schedule, a list of materials and tools, and a construction videotape. The contractors and all fitting and finish materials are the homeowner's responsibility.

The final cost will run from about $75,000 to $120,000, depending on the area of the country and the choice of finishes, but at well under $150,000, it is a clear bargain for such a sleek, elegant design. For a $10,000 retainer, plans, instructions, and a checklist of things to do for the preparation of the house are sent that allow the homeowner and contractor to lay the foundation and prepare for the construction of the materials, which will arrive in a minimum of about 21 days later, depending on how long the waiting list is with other customers. Assuming there are no interruptions (an assumption almost never satisfied in the construction of standard homes), contractors should be able to finish the house in a month or two; the house has been designed to be easily put together by two to four people. The fact that the shell, which should take a matter of a week or even days to assemble, will already be in place when finishing the inside helps enormously with weather conditions; everything can be done without worrying about rain or wind or snow.

Romero's website includes an 11-page list of the most frequently asked questions from her customers, such as "What is Galvalume, with which the exterior is sided?" (aluminum-coated tin) and "Is the roof built with a pitch, for runoff?" (yes, a half-inch valley at the end of the roof guides water to two downspouts). Here, those interested in exploring the home can find out everything from how to overcome the stigma of prefab when applying for a traditional mortgage to what building codes the home has incorporated in its design. A model of the home can be viewed near the manufacturing plant in Perryville, Missouri, about an hour south of St. Louis, which shows the higher-end finishing of the house, with a flat-screen television and sophisticated stereo system, for example. This version of the home cost $113,315 to produce, all of which is detailed in a list on the website so that homeowners will get an idea of the process involved in finishing it.

There is only one structural wall in the house, between the living area and bedrooms, so it can be arranged for other uses or designed in other ways internally by the homeowner. Though not designed to be attached, two or more LV homes might be used to create a bigger house area, perhaps joined by a courtyard or connected by covered patios. The house may also be shipped outside the United States after clearing local zoning codes. The Laguna Verde location is a perfect example of why prefab works so well for second homes—the materials can be shipped to remote sites with little trouble.

In addition to having an inspirational design, one that Romero credits to the influence of Mies van der Rohe, the house is extremely well engineered, with six-inch exterior walls making it energy efficient and quiet. It also passes some of the strictest national codes, including those for high wind, snow, and earthquake zones.

In a similar way, Romero has also designed the Fish Camp House. This prefab "camp structure," as she terms it, is simple, stylish, and easy to build. Calling it

"an elegant tent," she designed it based on her and her husband's experience of wanting to spend weekends by a stream and needing a place to stay. It was built to be so basic that "if it washes away, it doesn't really matter," jokes Romero. ■

LEFT and **ABOVE**: The Fish Camp House is another complete kit house that is intended as a second home for the woods or a remote area in which to campout. It is at the same time makeshift yet modern, rustic yet comfortable. The interior opens up to the landscape with large sliding doors.

jennifer siegal

SEATRAIN HOUSE | PORTABLE HOUSE | SWELLHOUSE

A quality admired in many prefab houses today is their adaptability—with mobile structures, especially, there is the literal ability to fit in almost anywhere. They are instant houses, but because much attention has been paid their to design, they have the comfort and warmth of homes. Jennifer Siegal created her Los Angeles architecture firm, the Office of Mobile Design, around the idea that mobility in buildings is good—and cost-effective, as well; it has just been the design and materials used in the past that have given the mobile home a bad name.

She has used this form to economic and social advantage. She has worked in South Africa to build affordable housing for people there; created the Eco Lab, taking a former furniture moving truck and turning it into a moving classroom that teaches kids about the environment; brainstormed the IMobile, a traveling technology system for people who don't have access to computers, like the elderly, less advantaged, and children. All of this has been done with appealing interiors and smart design.

Although her latest project is not literally portable, it makes a peripatetic lifestyle possible. Her client, Richard Carlson, is semiretired and travels six months of the year, so he wanted a house that would be easy to maintain and to leave behind. In response, Siegal created the Seatrain House, made simply from four 40-foot steel-and-aluminum shipping containers surrounded by a glass facade and topped with a metal roof. The containers create a sense of mobility and change, not only because of their past lives as vehicles to transport things from one place to another, but because they are easy to move from wherever they are found (usually "littering the byways like used soda cans," as Carlson says) and are simple to alter and customize to the new purpose. The containers were built with care—they were made to be durable and many of them even have mahogany floors. "They are the building blocks of the construction industry," says Siegal, becoming the latest thing for architects and designers to work

LEFT: The Seatrain House in Los Angeles was created from four shipping containers that are surrounded by glass and covered with a metal roof. Painted a dark olive color on the outside, the containers fit into the junglelike landscape of mango and guava trees. When the wind blows the trees next to the house, there is a wonderful brushing sound against the containers.

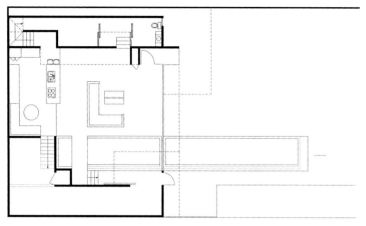

SEATRAIN HOUSE, FIRST FLOOR

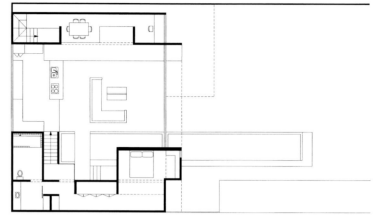

SEATRAIN HOUSE, SECOND FLOOR

with, supporting both the surge in prefab and the broader recycling of materials.

For the Seatrain House in Los Angeles, the containers have been easily constructed to form a 3,000-square-foot home for $150,000 (although Siegal estimates the house would cost about $300,000 to replicate because Carlson used so many salvaged materials for the house). Two stacked containers form a 1,280-square-foot living area, and others were carved to make separate rooms like an office and a

ABOVE and RIGHT: A glass bridge on the second story of the house keeps the more private rooms separate from the more public part of the house. An indoor lap pool is made from, of course, a shipping container. A smaller glass bridge across the pool echoes the larger one above it.

bedroom. There is even a lap pool made from one container lined with three coats of black epoxy pool paint and a goldfish pond constructed from part of another. Far from being just utilitarian structures for building, the containers in this house are loved for what they are. Hatch pulls, flap gates, rivets that *The New York Times* compared to decorative molding, and large-letter stenciling are still visible beyond the green and yellow colors used to paint them. Some, near the landscaping, were painted dark olive to blend in with the mango and guava trees, and the foliage of one of the trees makes brushing sounds against the steel. In Carlson's bedroom, the rust patina from the container was left as the natural wall covering. Carlson speaks affectionately of the containers, saying that though they do heat up in the sun of California, it reminds him of the comforting heat from warm rocks after a cold swim. The containers

... the house from ... their strength ... special-
izes ... fact,
created ... er-
national a ...
"the poverty ...
ways—by puttin...
the interior, and us...
rials. The idea is to c... ...ce in a
very basic form.

LEFT: The owner of the Seatrain House, Richard Carlson, is a fan of found objects, so a house of shipping containers was a natural draw. The wood beams of the house were taken from a Burbank shipping plant. ABOVE: The interiors were designed by David Mocarski to be easily maintained and longlasting, and include ultrasuede furniture and granite kitchen counters.

jennifer siegal

ABOVE: Corrugated metal roofs fit with the character of the Seatrain House, as does the slate of the master bath. RIGHT: On the interiors, the shipping containers were painted in greens and yellows, echoing the gardens outside. "You can't go wrong with the colors from nature," says Carlson.

The house is made of a shipping container frame and is 40 feet by 12 feet. It is actually a box within a box—when a button is pushed, a built-in hydraulic system extends one, adding 10 more feet of living space. There is a central kitchen and bath area, with sleeping spaces on one side and the expandable living space on the other. The expandable space is translucent to let in light and the structure as a whole looks like a regular house with picture windows. The entire structure can be put in different places to take in the best natural light and airflow.

The materials are much more cutting-edge than those used in most other mobile homes, or most standard homes, for that matter. They are hip in design and environmentally aware, from the structural wall panels that result in lower energy use to the "plastic" walls, which are actually Homasote, a terrifically insulated siding made from recycled paper that, in its production, causes less air pollution and uses up to 70 percent less water and up to 70 percent less energy than plastic. The floors are made of Plyboo, a laminated bamboo product that saves trees. A radiant electric heater keeps the house warm but uses 50 percent less wattage than traditional floor heaters, and hot water flows through the house, not from a tank.

"People look at it as either a first home, an addition to a home, or a separate studio space—an accessory that can be plugged into an existing situation," says Siegal. "It's off-the-shelf housing but the design still comes through." These structures can also

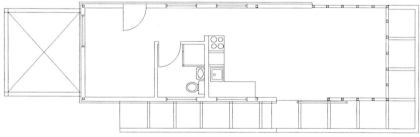

PORTABLE HOUSE

ABOVE: The Portable House fits right in with what *Hwy 111* magazine calls, "the movement Movement," today's tendency to be mobile in homeowning but with great design. RIGHT: The Swellhouse offers a spacious, affordable version of the American home, with "smart" materials.

be put together to provide a bigger house, or stacked, which is Siegal's preference. She has studied the philosophy of Paolo Soleri and his Arcosanti project and, like Soleri, believes in the idea of vertical living.

Siegal believes that mobile houses fit the way people live today; she calls our generation "the new nomads," with all the mobility that computers have brought us, and she draws connections from current lifestyles back to those Bedouin tribes and all the other nomads throughout history. Some of this mobile thinking is natural to her because of her background; her grandfather owned a hot dog cart on Coney Island and she ran one to put herself through school. Later, while in Israel she saw a portable gas station that could be folded up and moved when needed because of economic and political changes. To her, the enormous potential for portability combined with good design seems obvious. "The technology and materials are available," she says, "but for some reason they're not being utilized." The Office of Mobile Design has contributed a new take on the bookmobile; a Portable Construction Training Center that teaches construction skills so that low-income housing can be built; and various mobile units that can be dispatched for charity work.

Siegal has also developed the Swellhouse, a project that recognizes, as she says, that "home ownership is the American dream, but for many it is a compromised dream when the only affordable choice is a prefab." This house changes that, allowing extensive choice and customization and while using prefab housing technologies and materials.

Designed with the framework of the human skeleton in mind, "S"-shaped modular structures are used for economy of movement, and bolted together at the factory. They are made with electrical, plumbing, and information technology already installed. There is a curtain wall of glass, which lets in light but uses the Ecology Sun System (ECOSS) to reduce heat from the sun with a series of acrylic bars and aluminum louvers. Sliding panels form interior courtyards, exterior decks, and entryway so that the outdoors is brought into the house. Materials include bamboo, slate, and concrete flooring, prefab steel stairs, and recycled glass. ■

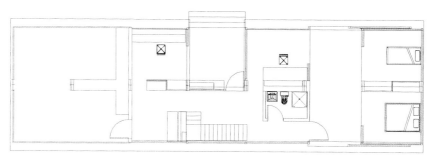

SWELLHOUSE, FIRST FLOOR

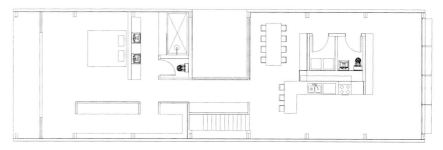

SWELLHOUSE, SECOND FLOOR

tim **pyne**

M - H O U S E

One of the things people love about many of today's prefab houses, it seems, is often the same thing that people love about stucco buildings—their honest, straightforward lines and simple forms, sitting easily on the land like part of the landscape, like trees. In the case of these prefab houses, however, they are exotic trees, with chic, hip, arresting designs.

The m-house (pronounced "mouse") is a prime example. There is something about its look that makes it seem very progressive but at the same time like it has been there—wherever "there" is—forever. What makes it more remarkable is that it is mobile. It is so mobile, in fact, it can be placed in the country, floated on water, sited on the roof of a city building, in a garden in back of a main house, or just about anywhere else. Because of its sleek simplicity, it fits in every place; it looks natural, as if it were planned for exactly the spot in which it is found. Or, as Patrick Dellew, professor of environmental engineering at Yale and head of the design firm Atelier 10 that is part of this effort, says, "It sits lightly on the earth."

RIGHT: The m-house is a full kit home that can be ordered online. The flat roof is one of the features that distinguishes it from traditional trailer designs. The exterior finish is customizable, with a choice of plain aluminum as shown, printed aluminum with chic checks or stripes, cedar strips or shingles, or painted tongue-and-groove wood.

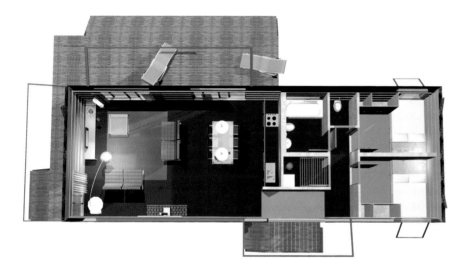

model, and received in 12 weeks, then put together in a day by two people Pyne sends. The house comes in just two pieces, which are then "zipped together" on the site. So the house could arrive in the morning and be ready in time for the owner to cook dinner in it. "We'll even put milk in the fridge," says Pyne, referring to the remarkable degree to which the luxury model is prefinished—arriving on the land that becomes its home that same day.

The designers—who, in addition to Pyne, include an ex-DJ, a lawyer, and an engineer—claim that the success of the house owes as much to product design as to building architecture, with every detail thought out. The distinctive awnings on the outside, for instance, are beautifully sewn to their steel frames. All this design input insures that the house is virtually maintenance-free and built to last at least 50 years. The house has a self-supporting steel structure, one of the key elements distinguishing it from traditional mobile homes. This frame allows for the 1,000-square-feet space to exist without interior walls, if the owner chooses, so the m-house can be used as an office or studio. Even with interior walls, which create two bedrooms and an open-plan living room, there is a loftlike feel. The luxury version is completely outfitted with Neff appliances in the kitchen, mosaic tiles in the bath, tongue-and-groove ceilings, a wood-burning stove, highest-standard insulation, under-floor heating, and a laundry room. A hot tub can be plumbed in for an extra cost.

The house came about because its designer, Tim Pyne, bought a plot of land in Essex, England, that only allowed mobile homes and then "saw there wasn't anything decent on the market." So he designed his own. Then his friends wanted one. Today, a m-house can be ordered from London for anywhere from $160,000 for the basic shell to $240,000 for the fully outfitted luxury

ABOVE: The two-bedroom home comes with the option of a wood deck. RIGHT: The house can be ordered as a shell or complete with interior finishes down to the faucets if the owner wants. The bedrooms come with built-in king-size beds and the baths with mosaic tiles. The top-grade materials and fixtures include Scandanavian windows and wool carpets.

Pyne used to work on a ship, so he knew planning the king-size beds and wardrobes in the bedrooms as built-ins would save space. They, along with the other furnishings and cabinetry, are made of birch. Only living and dining furniture have to be supplied by the owner. There is a choice of finishes that include black linoleum in the kitchen, wool carpet in the bedroom, and for the exterior of the house, a plain or check-print aluminum, cedar strip or shingles, or tongue-and-groove wood. The company's website allows consumers to click on to different finishes to see what the house looks like in a variety of guises. Most importantly, says Mike Howe, one of the design partners, is that "the language" of the mobile home is gone. One small example is that the windows and doors are domestic timber, like a regular house.

Pyne consulted with all sorts of experts for this venture, from financial advisors to one of the few specialists in mobile home planning law. The design partners' diverse backgrounds account for both the uniqueness and the adaptability of the house. People who buy a m-house—and a few are already starting to be seen around Colorado—receive all-inclusive advice on financing, legal issues, insurance, and even landscape design.

In addition to making a home affordable, Pyne sees other advantages to the house. It allows quality control since it is built onsite at the firm's factory, often by workers who have experience in ship building and other heavy industries that barely

exist in their cities and towns in England anymore. So the labor is prime and badly needed jobs are supplied for these skilled workers. Plus, there is an environmental benefit—the land doesn't have to get dug into and damaged since the house sits on top of it. "It's almost like parking a car," says Pyne. It sounds like trailer life, but by this time, one has nearly forgotten that this is a mobile home. Trailer chic—who would ever have guessed? ■

ABOVE and RIGHT: The house is a clear departure from trailer living. Mike Howe, who helped design the m-house, says, "We want the interior to feel like loft living. We feel that it should be homely, but ordered." Pyne surrounded himself with experts when designing the house, including an exhibition contractor so that the structures would be built on time.

first penthouse

There is probably no greater proof of the diversity of prefab housing today than the fact that there are prefab penthouses. To see these ultraluxurious structures on the top of some of most chic and prestigious buildings in London (and soon, New York) is to realize how far prefab has come. In fact, for London's recent Albert Court penthouses, which overlook Albert Hall, no less than Sotheby's International marketed the units. When an agent took a potential buyer on a viewing to see where his penthouse would sit, the buyer thought the plywood construction huts on the roof, which were there while pipes were being fixed, were the penthouse buildings themselves because of the bad reputation of prefab.

Nothing could be less like these structures created by First Penthouse. The Swedish company is using the same Scandanavian technology that made the largest sailing ship in the world to build homes with leather carpeting, marble floors, complete stereo systems, and stunning views. Because of the long Scandanavian winters, cabins for the ship were constructed indoors and then craned in individually. In a similar way, the company is making the penthouses in modules, shipping them to the United States or Great Britain, and having them lifted by crane, some-

times to incredible heights. In one day, a new penthouse is installed, complete with electricity, central heating and air, and plumbing.

There is a reason that *Architecture* magazine calls this "luxury in a box." The elements, finishes, and interior design are absolutely distinctive, including window walls, wood-burning fireplaces, roof gardens, high-design tile, and under-floor heating. Everything, down to the light switches and the paint on the walls, is done in the factory before the modules arrive onsite. All of these specifications are designed by the clients over a computer in the planning stages of the structure. To save money, they can have some of the finishing done themselves. Or they can go the other way and order whatever they want— a feng shui floor plan or an elaborate entertainment system. Depending on these elements, the cost is

LEFT: The arched-window penthouses that now top the illustrious Albert Court in London are actually prefab structures that were made in a factory in Sweden and craned to the top of the building. The fact that they blend in so well with the architecture of the historic building is a reason for their success.

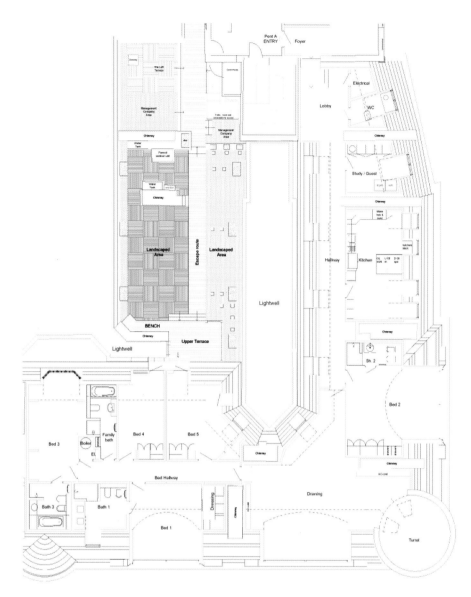

ABOVE: The four- to five-million-dollar structure represent a significant departure from prefab housing of the past. The space alone is impressive, with several bedrooms and baths, a lightwell, and a huge area for a garden. **RIGHT**: The opulence continues in the detailing, with arches and niches plus high-end wood floors and built-in fireplaces.

about four to five million dollars for a three-bedroom, three-bath, 3,800-square-foot loft. Even this is half the cost of some of the estimates for a newly built structure. And much smaller structures of about 350 square feet, for adding a room perhaps, sell for about $200,000.

After the design is in place, the roof of the building is prepared in London or New York while the modules are being built at a factory in Sweden, the same one that makes outlets for McDonald's, interestingly enough. The roof preparation takes about five or six weeks, but even for this part of the process, which may include rebuilding chimneys, rerouting vents, and building a substructure, quiet tools like diamond-core drills are used to reduce noise. After about 10 weeks, when the 14-ton modules arrive in London or New York, they are engineered by crane so carefully that wind patterns for the day are researched and taken into account. The modules are connected and a strip of wood for the flooring or window for the exterior walls covers the connecting point. It is only through 3-D computer design and the precision of the Swedish system that such success could be attained. Installation is usually completed in one day, and it takes another three or four weeks for exterior and interior finishes to be completed.

It is this ease of installation that is making these lofty residences possible, because there is hardly any construction interference or scaffolding,

no dust, very little noise—in short, no neighbors complaining and no vetoes from building boards. Regular building would likely be denied because of the time and trouble it causes everyone. The company also achieves permission to add to these buildings with updates to the pipes, insulation, and other fixtures, a real draw in cities like London and New York where the fixtures are often antiquated. The design for each penthouse is different, made in line with the architecture of the building, so it is a beautifully drawn, respectful look, one that tends to meet with the approval of architects and historical societies.

"The big challenge is to make it look like there has always been a penthouse," says Annika Olsson, a civil engineer, as is her husband, Hakan. Together they started First Penthouse after seeing what a hassle construction to their own home proved to be. At Albert Court the new arched-window rooftops belong as naturally to the period building as the turrets and other elements that are part of the original. This effect is due both to the aesthetic of the design and to the Olsson's painstaking care for preservation. For example, some of the original tiles from the mansard-style roof were taken off the old building at Albert Court and shipped to the factory in Sweden to be put onto the new one. ■

RIGHT: Everything, down to the light switches, is installed in the factory before the modules are shipped and put together in their final location. The arched windows at Albert Court are essential not only to the high design and light of the space, but so that the penthouses fit in with the original architecture of the building.

oskar leo kaufmann

When photographer Matthew Hranek and his wife, Yolande, were ready to build a house on their 130-acre plot in Sullivan County, New York, he sent out an e-mail. He dispatched the details of his building site and budget (about $150,000) to an Austrian architect in the forefront of prefab design. The designer, Oskar Kaufmann, e-mailed back a picture of what the house, a model called SU-SI, would look like—a 1,400-square-foot glass alpine box with three bedrooms and two bathrooms that could be assembled in about five days. The bill: $145,100. Although Hranek would have to do some prep work, it was exactly what the couple wanted. "We could never have had this built with these materials for this cost," says Hranek. "We're getting a half-million-dollar house for under $200,000 with incredible European materials, insulation, finishes, and windows." Although he had to sort out some details, such as finding out whether Austrian and U.S. building codes clashed, it was a small obstacle. "That's what it takes to be a pioneer, I guess."

The Hraneks' new home is the first Kaufmann and his firm KFN Products have shipped to the United States, but there's a waiting list of more than one hundred stateside customers. Oskar Kaufmann formed KFN with his cousin Johannes Kaufmann in 1997 and it only took them a year to achieve prefab fame. Their first success came in 1998 when Oskar's sister, Suzy Kaufmann, needed a place to live. For Suzy he created the first SU-SI house, its name a play on hers.

The transportable home manages to be sophisticated and sparely elegant, even though it was designed to be shipped on a flatbed truck and can be assembled in hours. SU-SI comes in different sizes, with options to customize both the interior and exterior. The house can even be placed on stilts, like a ski lodge, so that a car can be stored underneath. Inside, pale wood interiors are airily spacious. Living and dining areas and a small kitchen are on one side, and a bedroom and bathroom on the other. Soon after Suzy moved into SU-SI, the house was

RIGHT: The SU-SI House is 1,400 square feet with three bedrooms and two baths, and can be assembled in five days. Just visible to the right of the front door in this night shot is the bar code that comes with the house, a joke from KFN about buying houses instantly in this prefab age. In fact, it only takes five weeks after ordering the house to receive it on site.

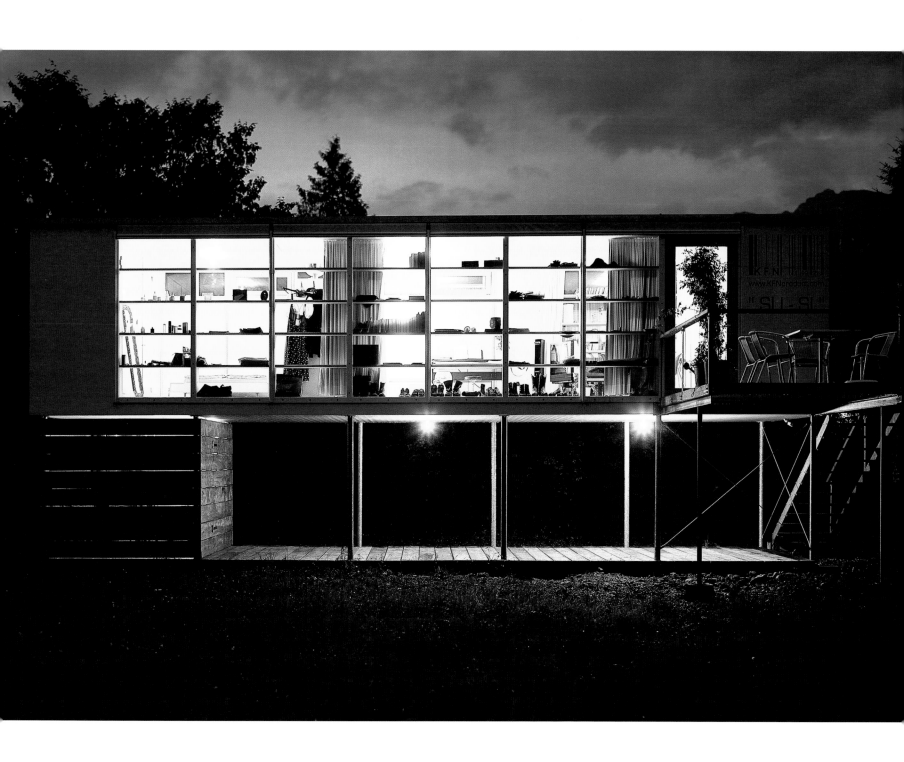

oskar leo kaufmann

featured in newspapers and magazines, and won KFN several design awards. Overnight, KFN found itself in the prefab business, selling 20 more houses in Austria and Germany in the next two years. On average, each buyer spent about $100,000, including shipping and foundation work.

KFN is also known for their FRED modular home-building system, a compact program. FRED, essentially a room unit that can be electronically expanded with controllable sliding walls, has been likened to a child's building blocks. The components of the unit come in different sizes, so they result in houses that vary in square footage. The modules can even be stacked up on top of each other. To create a sturdy unit, the modules are solidly built of quality materials. Using wood and glass as the only surfaces creates a lean yet well-grounded impression. The unit's big glass front invites plenty of daylight, while the well-insulated windows lower energy consumption, which is already kept down by the thick insulation in the walls, the roof, and the floor.

Because FRED is so small, relocating the structure by truck is not complicated. After FRED arrives at its destination, it can be assembled in as few as two hours. The owner can easily connect it to water and electricity sources, and it is quickly ready for habitation. Furniture and other needed items can be packed and transported within the container/unit.

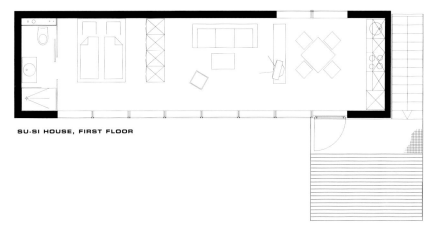

SU-SI HOUSE, FIRST FLOOR

LEFT and ABOVE: The SU-SI House is filled with space and fine materials. Even the ceilings are quality wood. Describing it as a "modern alpine box, more Breuer than Mies," owner Matthew Hranek says it is exactly what he wanted. It cost him less than $150,000.

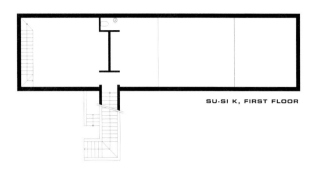

SU-SI K, FIRST FLOOR

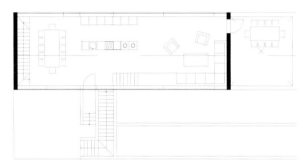

SU-SI K, SECOND FLOOR

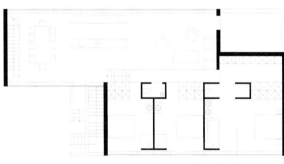

SU-SI K, THIRD FLOOR

ABOVE: The SU-SI K is a variation on the SU-SI. Both were created from KFN's OA.SYS, which stands for "Open Architecture System." The system consists of panels and planes that can be mixed and matched into different designs. TOP RIGHT: This design allowed for three stories and a lot of space. BOTTOM RIGHT: Interiors can be almost infinitely customized, like this all-white one.

oskar leo kaufmann

KFN also applies their innovative methods of prefabrication to houses that appear more conventional. There is the Two-Family House, an energy-efficient, timber-frame home. The frame, plus kitchen and bath units, are made offsite and the entire structure is ready in four months. In 2002, Oskar Kaufmann and fellow Austrian architect Johannes Norlander launched two customizable prototypes for these wood-frame houses. Both houses were installed onsite for a total cost of $400,000.

The Two-Family House uses a modular timber-frame construction. Modules can be combined as needed to create a house of up to four floors. The exterior is constructed from factory-produced walls. Customized finishing touches can be requested, much as when purchasing a new car.

For KFN, prefab is part of a growing and logical trend. People who have experienced the ease and mobility of shopping online will find prefabricated construction all the more appealing. After ordering clothes, books, and vitamins online, home buyers can send an e-mail about a house, get an e-mail back with a picture of what that house will look like, and have that house delivered to their door, or perhaps more accurately, the spot where their door will be. And it's exactly what they wanted for the amount they were ready to spend. ■

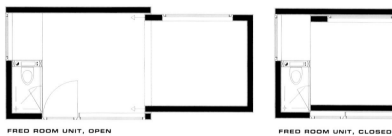

FRED ROOM UNIT, OPEN　　　　　　　FRED ROOM UNIT, CLOSED

ABOVE: The FRED expands when the walls slide electronically, adding another area to the studio house; it can also be used as a workplace. It takes five weeks to arrive from the time of ordering, and two hours to install after it is shipped on the back of a truck. RIGHT: The Two-Family House is KFN's less portable prefab option, but was still built in only four months.

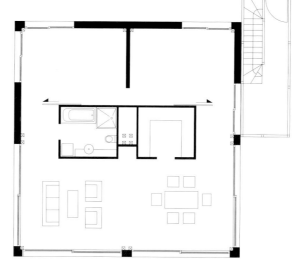

TWO-FAMILY HOUSE: FIRST AND SECOND FLOOR

LEFT and ABOVE: All of the parts of the Two-Family House, including the kitchen and baths, were made in a shop and installed onsite. The cost was a total of about $400,000, a clear bargain for two homes. KFN worked with the owners to determine the size and layout of the house.

oskar leo kaufmann

david hertz

Much of today's prefab is wonderfully creative because of situational limitations on what can be built. With limitations often come creative solutions, solutions that not only solve an immediate problem, but also help create a distinctive, edgy contemporary building. Say you start with a small urban corner lot that's only 30-odd feet wide and 80 feet long and a firm budget of $270,000. These were the limitations faced by the Hesses, a professional couple in Venice, California. The couple, who owned the property, asked architect David Hertz to design a home that would fit in these parameters and house not only themselves, but a grandparent and two teenage children. The couple also wanted separate studios in which to conduct their business. That meant four bedrooms, two studios, one family den, three and a half bath-

RIGHT: **To accommodate a narrow corner lot, the house was made from concrete panels that were tilted up to join (one can see the interlocking of the panels on the right side of the building). Eleven panels were made offsite and three onsite, and were joined in just 10 hours to form the exterior of the house. Windows and doors are storefront aluminum that were customized.**

rooms, a living area, a kitchen and dining area, and a two-car garage. With five occupants, the nature of the space's mixed use, and its bustling urban setting, noise and privacy were also important issues. The home's many functions meant there had to be enough space so that business, for example, did not intrude on daily life. The site's noisy urban location meant there had to be some physical separation between the house and nearby structures.

To meet these challenging limitations with style, Hertz created the innovative Tilt-Up Slab House, which he describes as a "mini high-rise." The design centers on an elongated interior space defined by concrete panels that face each other. To create this space, Hertz enclosed it with 14 six-inch-thick tilt-up white concrete panels lined up along the longitudinal edges of the site. A very efficient way to enclose space on a large scale, a similar tilt-up methodology is sometimes used in warehouses. Scaling the technique down made it livable.

Using prefabricated building techniques to customize this project was the right solution for the award-winning architect, who often uses unusual materials, such as Syndecrete, a precast lightweight concrete surfacing material, to build works that are

uniquely suited to the specifics of their sites. In this site, concrete panels were also a practical consideration. Wood would have been impractical, vulnerable to moisture, dry rot, mold and termites. Concrete panels, which require minimal maintenance, were also an ideal solution for a busy household. They don't require painting, and are very durable—a selling point on a busy corner where cars sometimes hit the site's previous structure.

The aesthetic simplicity of the concrete panels also makes for an honest design statement of what the building is all about—inside and out. The lot's corner location leaves one of the longitudinal sides exposed, revealing the distinctive structure and connections between the panels. The interior side of the panels was also left exposed, hand sanded, sealed, and waxed to preserve their spare beauty. In their simplicity, the walls seem to shimmer in the indirect light. A white cement plaster finish is applied to shower and tub surfaces. The floor is a reflective burnished concrete and fixtures are minimal.

Creating this unique structure was an object lesson in why prefab is increasingly popular. Much of the building arrived in a truck and was assembled quickly. Eleven of the panels were poured offsite and then hauled in by truck while three panels were poured onsite and placed in position by connecting them to the structural steel. Using this construction method made it possible to have all the panels erected in just 10 hours—less than a day from building site to building. According to Hertz, pouring some of the panels offsite not only cut down on time but also helped cut down dramatically on costs, keeping the house within budget.

To ensure privacy and tone down the tumult of outside noise, windows on the Tilt-Up Slab House were kept to a minimum, giving it a gritty, urban edge. Natural light and ventilation enter through the almost entirely glazed front facade, through the rear, and through the central, double-height atrium, which culminates in an operable skylight. Despite its economic use of windows, the house seems to glow with light. The windows and doors that were included in the design are cus-tomized storefront aluminum, which when opened seem to disappear from inside view, projecting entirely to the outside. An internal 10-foot court-yard separates the garage building from the rest of the house. Inside, the concrete flooring contains radiant heating, powered through rooftop solar panels, keeping the home at an ideal temperature while using minimal outside energy.

Hertz is highly regarded for his ability to provide comfort of shelter while maintaining a strong connec-tion to the home's exterior. Sometimes the smartest way to achieve these things, and everything else a homeowner could desire, in one space-efficient, budget-conscious project is to think prefab. ▪

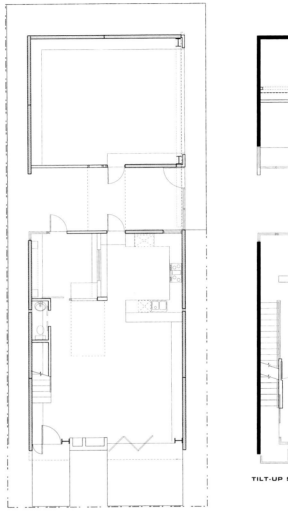

TILT-UP SLAB HOUSE, FIRST FLOOR

TILT-UP SLAB HOUSE, SECOND FLOOR

LEFT: The interiors of the concrete panels were polished and sealed so they could be left as elegant inside walls. The floors are burnished concrete. ABOVE: A 10-foot courtyard was placed in the center of the structure to provide openness on the nar-row lot and separate different areas of the house.

collins and turner

Some of the prefab houses made today are so beautifully designed that they end up looking like works of art, perhaps because of the necessay use of simple forms and the resulting elegant lines. In the case of the houses that Collins and Turner Architects have created, the starting point actually is art, as their inspiration comes from the minimalist landscape sculptures of Donald Judd. For the Bombala Farmhouse, a home in the Monaro plains of New South Wales in Australia, Penelope Collins and Huw Turner built on what Turner calls "Judd's idea of a specific object, a precision abstract form, set in a barren landscape. In the end, only the abstract forms and landscape are to be remembered." That is indeed what is remembered—the lines of the land, the lines of the house. It is a won-

RIGHT: The Bombala Farmhouse was built on a 3,000-acre farm for a family in New South Wales, Australia. The trees on the property create as much of a profile as the house, which complements their form. The skeleton is steel to support the glass walls, and the exterior is made of corrugated metal siding and aluminum, all of which will last for years with little care.

derful notion to live in a piece of art, amid the natural art of the surrounding landscape.

What is just as wonderful, however, is that it works. The house is an intimate and comfortable place inside, with a poetic minimalism due to the decorative elements and finishes used, and the way in which the outside is brought close via walls of glass allowing for expansive views of the water, the hills, and the bush. Most important to the house's success however, is the fact that it is prefab. The Monaro plains are remote—the nearest skilled labor six hours away by car in Sydney—so even furniture was made offsite and brought in. Turner says prefab inspired more creativity, not less: "The knowledge that we could fabricate parts of the building in a controlled factory environment and then transport them in a protected state . . . allowed us to think more freely about the design."

The prefab materials also made sense for the actual function of the building in many ways. Both the lightness and strength of a steel structure was ideal for supporting the heavy window walls that cover so much of the structure. The exteriors, corrugated metal siding, aluminum, and glass are all materials that last a long time and age well. Indoors,

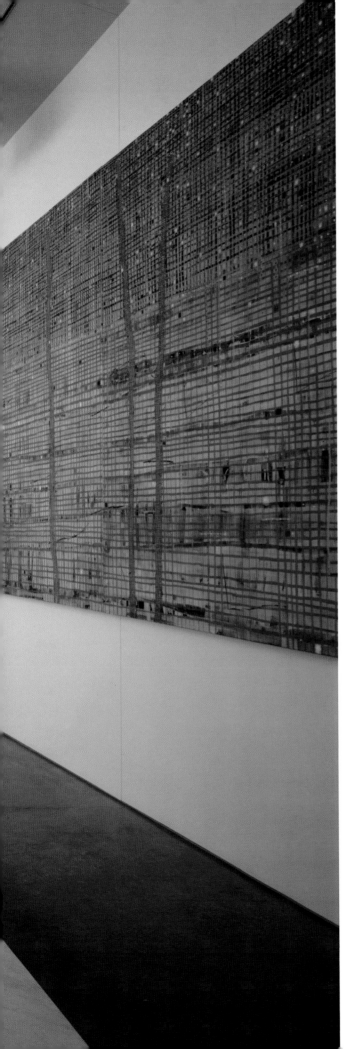

the significant amount of glass acts as a solar heater for cool winters, and the concrete floors store that heat from the sun naturally, further warming up the house and saving it for cold nights. There is also under-floor heating in case the sun isn't out. Other materials that Turner calls "self-finishing," like stainless steel and glass, were also used for the indoors. On an environmental note, rainwater is collected from the roof and kept in a tank underground.

LEFT and **ABOVE**: The interior is as streamlined as the outside of the house. Cupboards were made to disappear into walls, baseboards are a thin aluminum line, and the materials are sleek—mostly concrete, stainless steel, and glass. Almost all parts of the house were made offsite and simply and quickly assembled at the remote farm.

The owner of the house requested that it look more like a farm shed than a traditional home, so Collins and Turner made it echo the agricultural architecture that gives character to the Morano landscape. "These are usually function-driven forms," describes Collins, "with no formal geometry; they lack reference to the human scale, and they tend to meet the ground in an indifferent manner. With its unusual proportions and its separation from the ground, the house evokes the surreal presence of these structures." To get what Collins calls "one house with two outlooks"—there is a serene hillside view on one side of the house and a dramatic view of the 3,000-acre farm on the other—the house was built with expanses of glass next to steel for privacy and enclosure on each side, with the reverse side flipped to steel and then glass. This provides both privacy and views on both sides. The vastness of the windows allows views through the structure, as well as outside of it. The fact that such an unusual structure, designed both specifically for the owner and the site, was created from prefab materials is another victory for prefab, and a promising development for anyone who is interested in buying a prefab house.

Collins and Turner used the Bombala Farmhouse as something of a template for their design of a

RIGHT: The Silverbox Homes series, which is available online, was inspired by the simple form of the Bombala Farmhouse. This is Wing, which is reminiscent of the sleek design of Japanese houses and is created for sunny climates, with an overhang to provide shade to the house.

line of small and medium prefab houses for the United States, called Silverbox Homes. Looking through the website for these may remind one of visiting an art gallery, since the homes have the same artistic feel as the farmhouse. Fairly inexpensive and of excellent quality, the houses all are created with views and open-plan living in mind. Window walls and sliding glass screens are used to create a relationship between the outdoors and indoors. The houses are either timber, in which case they are made of insulated panels, a prefab element that packs flat and is easily put together, or metal, using recycled-grade alloy frames.

The Silverbox comes in five different innovative and beautiful styles. The Lantern model, which is currently being made for a site in Grass Valley, California, is named for its high clerestory windows that sit above the central rooms. Motorized louvers and sun blinds above these "lanterns" control the light and heat levels in the house during the day. Living areas run into terraces to take advantage of mild climates, making possible large spaces that join the indoors and out. Collins says the design "celebrates the lightness and elegance of metal-framed construction." Unique materials like recycled rubber tires for a roof membrane, cork and rubber flooring, strawboard ceilings, and other simple prefab elements add an environmental component. Customization includes a choice of finishes and options such as wool carpets, stainless steel kitchens, and translucent white glass screens to divide bedrooms from baths. The number of bedrooms ranges from one to three depending on the model.

Wing, so named because of the dramatic aluminum roof that overhangs the glass structure below, is designed to shield the house from the sun in hot climates. Inspired by traditional Japanese houses, the interior finishes are similar to Lantern's, with cupboards and closets that disappear into walls.

Shed is intended as a weekend house, but one that is built to last, with recreation-ready finishes such as vinyl floors and cement wall paneling.

Veil is a new version of the log home, with traditional timber on the outside but frameless windows and high-design finishes. A screen of fine timber slats provides a fringe for filtering sunlight. Inside, the space is large, open, and fluid, but with log walls—contemporary detailing keeps them minimalist and spare.

Peak takes classic barn architecture and makes it absolutely contemporary. Zinc roof sheets lend elegance, and exterior walls are stained timber. Inside Douglas fir is used for floors and ceilings to create a sense of warmth that contrasts with the stainless steel and opal glass in the kitchen. In the bathrooms, panels in aluminum frames bring in light but are placed for privacy. A suite of four bedrooms leads off to a continuous roof terrace that goes across one side of the house, and there is a gym and study area. Large sliding screens hide hallways, the laundry area, and bathrooms, and the wardrobes are built in. To top it off, the lights are computer controlled.

Being able to choose between these kinds of houses from a website is what prefab is all about today—a place few thought it would ever be. ■

LEFT: Lantern, another home in the Silverbox series, has surrounding clerestory windows or "lanterns" to bring daylight to all parts of the house. It is made in modules with a lightweight alloy frame and precast concrete floors, compressed strawboard ceilings, and aluminum and glass walls.

anderson anderson **architecture**

The triumph of prefab is that it can make houses possible for people who might have trouble affording them otherwise; the miracle of it is that those houses can be great designs. Today's prefab not only asserts that housing is a democratic ideal—that people should be able to have them without going broke—but that good design is democratic, as well. By their very nature, these houses declare that good design is not the exclusive possession of anyone, but is rather an aesthetic integrated into society that is available to almost all.

Melissa Kennedy is a firefighter in Washington state who came to Anderson Anderson Architecture with a budget of under $120,000 for a new house on Fox Island, near Seattle. With all the disheartening reports from around the country over the years that fire and police department employees often cannot afford to live in the districts they serve, it is refreshing to see that Melissa Kennedy got her house for her budget. And it is a distinctive home, rich in bright and beautiful materials and, though prefab, personally designed for Kennedy and for the site.

Peter and Mark Anderson, brothers who have a background in building, saw that it was prefab that would cut costs and allow a house on the hilly lot. There was no room on the hill for all the things and people used to construct a traditional house; with the Andersons' prefab system, however, a house's frame can come right to the site and be put up in pieces, in this case in just eight hours. The piece system—based on inexpensive panels of insulated Styrofoam encased in plywood—also saves money because building on location is "like making a factory on the site every day," says Peter. Offsite, the panels can be put together efficiently and inexpensively in a setting like a production line, no matter what the weather. The eight-foot-wide vertical panels can work on any kind of terrain because they are all level at the main floor, but can be lengthened or shortened below to adapt to different slopes.

The Andersons' system is distinct from a prefab house that is designed one way and sent to the client. With the system, there is a menu of components that can be changed around to accommodate different

LEFT: The Kennedy house is built with the architects' "mass-customization" system. The prefabricated panels, which were put together about 10 miles from the site, reach to the slope of the hill, since the panels can be made in different lengths depending on each building's need.

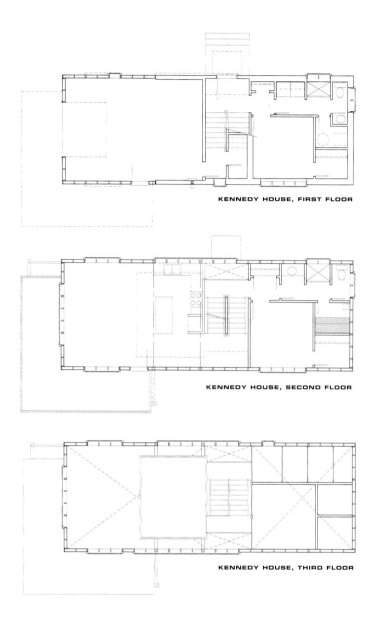

KENNEDY HOUSE, FIRST FLOOR

KENNEDY HOUSE, SECOND FLOOR

KENNEDY HOUSE, THIRD FLOOR

ABOVE: Inside, the house is roomy, partly due to the "balloon frame" construction that provides an arching roof. **RIGHT:** The open plan makes the house feel bigger than it is; simple, natural materials give it an honest, warm quality, particularly with the wood finish continuing to the ceiling.

lifestyles and different regions, effectively permitting the creation of different houses. A house can be made larger or smaller, with varying wings, and in different finishes. Because they are attached to the outside of the frame after it is already in place, the windows can be maneuvered around after the panel system is put up to allow a choice of views before final installation.

It is not only the design of the house that was customized, but the actual production of it, too. The Andersons made it possible for Kennedy to save more than $40,000 by doing some of the work herself, with the help of friends and family. "All I remember is standing, my brother-in-law, Dad, myself, and a friend of my brother-in-law, nailing away," she says of the siding that they put on, which was ingeniously adapted by the Andersons using asphalt-roll roofing in two colors and alternating them. Knowing that Kennedy's stepfather is a Navy welder, the Andersons fashioned all the steel handrails and beams to be welded with ship techniques so he could do the metalwork. They even installed a chin-up bar for Kennedy at the end of the kitchen so that she can keep fit for protecting other people's buildings.

The stylish balloon shape of the house rings a playful tone that is answered with the striped exterior and colorful doors and balcony, putting a personal touch to prefab and making sure that it is anything but bland or studious. But the balloon shape is also functional, allowing the ceiling of the house to rise gradually from either side and support an open plan

indoors, with 18-foot ceilings that make the 1,100 square feet of space seem bigger. Inside, the house is like a forest, with construction-grade wood bringing a lot of warmth to the two-bedroom structure, another cost-saving measure that feels instead like a rediscovery of a material. The storefront windows, as Peter calls them, are standard aluminum window frames first placed sideways and then on top of one another in threes, creating one large window for open views.

All of these standard materials are chosen not only for cost-effectiveness but also so that they can be found in Nebraska or Louisiana, Vermont or California, so that the prefab house system can be used throughout the country, although the total cost of the house can vary greatly depending on the location. And it is nothing if not practical. When her dog chewed off a piece of the siding, Kennedy just cut it out and replaced it with a new piece of the asphalt-roll roof. After all, she already knew how to install it.

Anderson Anderson has developed a very different kind of prefab housing system with the Cantilever House, the prototypes of which are being built as private homes—one in a scenic area near Granite Falls, outside Seattle, and one in an urban area in San Diego—to show how adaptable the system is to a variety of environments. Again, panels of insu-

lated Styrofoam and plywood or plasterboard are used, but in this system they work for the entire structure of the house—floors, walls, and roof. With their minimal labor requirements, the panels save huge amounts of time and expense. The other part of the structure is provided by a prefabricated steel frame.

Another brilliant aspect of this prefab system is the ease with which its foundation or footprint can be changed to fit the site. In the case of the four-bedroom Granite Falls house, the ground floor and foundation of the house was built very small, so that the house is touching a minimum of ground. Because the site is an outcropping of rock, the foundation would otherwise be incredibly expensive to install. The small foundation also has an environmental benefit—only a small portion of the natural land is touched by it.

As with the Kennedy house, the Andersons here use materials in a progressive way so that they seem new, while at the same time saving money. For example, the floors are concrete slabs (with heating underneath them), which happen to create a wonderful look, the kind that inspires a trend. Depending upon what area of the country the system is used, a house will cost an average of just under $100 a square foot, meaning a pretty high-end building can be bought for relatively little money. Though based on a system, each building is individualized for its location. In the case of the Granite Falls house, the roof is covered with soil, clover, and wildflowers to be completely at home with the site. ▪

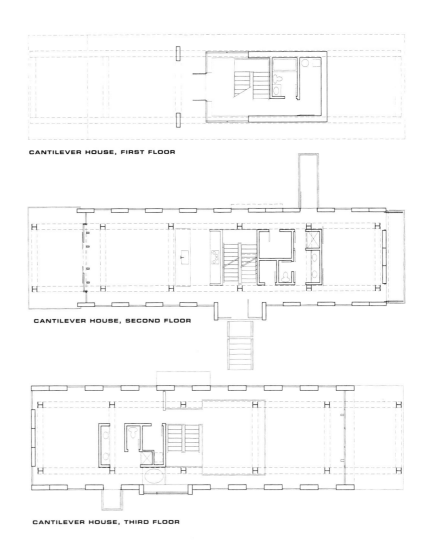

CANTILEVER HOUSE, FIRST FLOOR

CANTILEVER HOUSE, SECOND FLOOR

CANTILEVER HOUSE, THIRD FLOOR

LEFT: The house is so customizable that the roof for one version that sits on an elevated piece of rocky land is covered with soil, clover, and wildflowers. ABOVE: The Cantilever House, which is being built on a couple of sites already, is a spacious version of a prefab structure that also uses panels.

steven holl

New York architect Steven Holl's Turbulence House is a striking example of the joining of high technology and prefab. Computers are one of the leading reasons why prefab's time has come. By their very nature, components of buildings made by computer are pre-fabricated because they are made in a factory. In turn, of course, prefab benefits significantly from computer technology—parts can be made that much faster by machines that are commanded by computer. In many regards, the pairing of computers and prefab is an absolute natural.

In the case of the Turbulence House, the design process and the manufacture of the pieces used to make the structure literally would not have been possible without computers. Holl used cutting-edge, 3-D computer drafting to create the unique form of the house. A. Zahner Company Architectural Metals, a sheet metal fabrication company in Kansas City, had their computers follow Holl's drawings to create the 31 metal pieces that make up the exterior form of the house. They used digital definition to form the distinct and intricate shape and character of each piece. "The computer has really opened up a hopeful dimension for the future of architecture," says Holl. "Turbulence House's complicated shapes and delicate details were all crafted by machines engaged in a cross-country digital dialogue. Our computers were able to talk directly to Zahner's." Much like Frank Gehry's buildings, this house looks as though it has leapt off the page—or screen—of an animation computer sketch; that's how intimately connected the design and the manufacture process are with the computer.

The prototype of the house—created for owners, Richard Tuttle and Mei Mei Berssenbrugge, a visual artist and a poet, living in a remote part of New Mexico—sits among the colors of the landscape like a large, shining sculpture. Turbulence House is so named because it sits atop a windy mesa; the wind blows through the center of the house, which was left empty to create a vortex for the purpose of drawing cooling air into the structure. "The structure looks like a natural arch that siphons the wind through," says Tuttle.

RIGHT: The original Turbulence House, particularly sitting where it does, is extremely sensitive to environmental concerns. The majority of the windows are faced to control heat gain, roof panels generate electricity, storm water is collected for irrigation, and there is a radiant floor heating system for cold desert nights.

"Amazingly, the house actually echoes buttes in a valley crossed by the same river that flows through our mesa." Holl likens the look of the house to the tip of an iceberg that indicates a much larger form below. The 900-square-foot house is mostly one large room, with a 300-square-foot sleeping loft above the kitchen and a place for writing in another part of the structure.

The 31 panels that form the exterior of the house were designed to fit into a 40-foot container for shipping, so the limit on width of any panel was eight feet. The panels range from 6 by 10 feet to 8 by 22 feet; the largest weighed more than a ton. Made of galvanized aluminum, the panels have flexible ribs spaced 14 inches apart to both give the panels structure and allow them to bend across the rounded form of the building. "They were developed by linking special engineering software directly to the machinery in the metal shop," says Holl. Computer-generated templates were created to ensure that the final product was perfect, and that no aluminum was wasted in making it. A. Zahner even started a website devoted to the project, on which they posted progress reports. Of the $300,000 budget for the house, $175,000 went toward the exterior.

In addition to the fact that the house cools itself in what can be a very hot climate, the house is "green" in other ways. Photovoltaic roof panels generate electricity for the house, there is a radiant floor heating system, and a cistern on the side of the house collects storm water from the roof, which is used to irrigate the site.

A second Turbulence House was created for an exhibit in Vicenza, Italy, that took place in a medieval structure and was devoted to the architecture of three eras—medieval, Renaissance, and digital. Like the work of art that it is, this Turbulence House now appropriately sits in a sculpture park in Italy. ■

resolution: 4 architecture

BEACH HOUSE | SUB-URBAN HOUSE | HOUSE IN THE WOODS | SUMMER RETREAT

The stereotype about prefab is that it creates houses all alike, all in a row. But the reality is that, instead of mass production being the driving force behind what is created, mass customization is much more often the approach. Within a system, an almost limitless number of designs and houses can be created, according to the individual buyer's needs, wants, and budget; the site; the region of the country; the climate; and the tastes of the moment.

One of the most important developers of such a system is a New York architecture firm called Resolution: 4 Architecture. What principals Joe Tanney and Robert Luntz call their "methodology" can be used to give life to a range of different and unique houses. "It's impossible that one home is right for everybody," says Tanney. With their system, the client enters a distinct world in which the elements the

architects offer become the creative tools that will be used to make the home that is right for them.

The main elements are modules that are prefabricated and brought in on a truck, thus restricting them to dimensions of 16 feet wide, 60 feet long, and 11 feet high. The architects' focus, then, was to design with individuality and distinction within those modules, what Tanney calls "thinking *inside* the box." The modules are separated into those for communal use—living, dining, kitchen areas; those for private use—bed and bath, office and media rooms; and accessory modules containing closets and storage and hallways. Each of these is referred to as a "bar," and the bars may be combined in dozens of different ways. When assembled, they are an aesthetically pleasing excercise in geometry, with all their various configurations and patterns. Resolution: 4 Architecture has developed 36 separate house design types with the use of one or two or three bars in combination with one another.

The Standard Bar design uses one 870-square-foot module to create two bedrooms and all other areas of a normal house. The roof is pitched in an inverted design allowing light in through the top. The firm's Beach House, which was built for a simple lifestyle—as Tanney says, "two guys and three dogs"—

RIGHT: The Standard Bar design uses one module to create two bedrooms and all other areas of a normal house. The Beach House is a variation of this design where one bar is elevated on a box to create a carport below. The house was further customized by using materials that have a strong relationship to the surrounding lanscape.

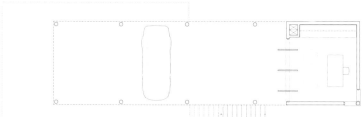

BEACH HOUSE, FIRST FLOOR

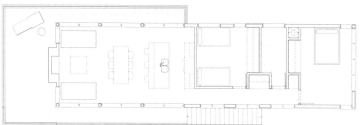

BEACH HOUSE, SECOND FLOOR

resolution: 4 architecture

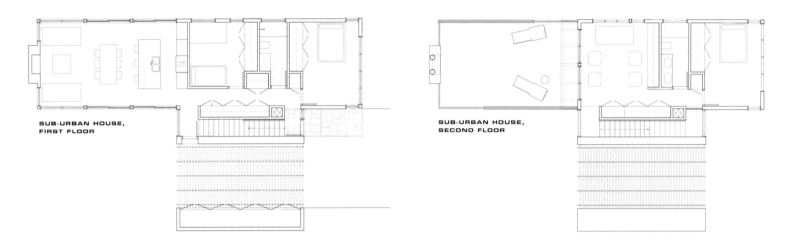

SUB-URBAN HOUSE,
FIRST FLOOR

SUB-URBAN HOUSE,
SECOND FLOOR

is a variation of this design. The module is set onto a small boxlike space on one end, in which sits an office, and lifted up by columns all along the rest of the module, creating a carport underneath. The living space is enclosed by glass and faces the water for views, and off of it is a balcony. "The materials have a strong relationship to the landscape," says Tanney, referring to the corrugated metal that echoes the color of the ocean and that was custom chosen for the house.

The Two-Story Bar doubles the space, with one module stacked on another. The firm's Sub-Urban

ABOVE and RIGHT: The plan for the Sub-Urban House shows how the Two-Story Bar system works. Private spaces and communal spaces are put in separate bars and then crossed at different places to create house designs, or smaller houses are created with one bar that is a module for prefabrication.

House is an example of this type, with 1,430 square feet and three bedrooms. As with most houses in the system, this one can be customized with an office, fourth bedrom, mudroom of 180 square feet, laundry room of 75 square feet, one- or two-car garage, poolhouse, wood deck, all kinds of storage and basement areas, and a media room or studio. As with much modern design, the aesthetic is in the space—what makes it beautiful is its simultaneous simplicity and utility.

Two-bar modules for houses make interesting designs because of the various ways space gets used and the different patterns that are created. When two modules intersect, for example, the space they create on the outside of the house can make right angles that form small courtyards, an attractive addition. In the case of Resolution: 4 Architecture's House in the Woods, a home they created for a North Carolina couple on a site surrounded by trees, a communal module was crossed with a private module, so one

wing contains public spaces and the other one more private spaces. Making the home meant using the communal and private modules and adding a stair module, storage module, and roof module. All modules were brought by truck to the site and placed onto a concrete foundation with a crane. This foundation contains all the mechanical systems for the house. Like other houses in the system, wood framing was used in combination with prefab elements already in use in other kinds of prefab buildings and adapted to this system. The home is customized with terraces on two sides and both floors of the house, a screened-in porch, and an outdoor shower to bring the owners that much closer to their landscape. Further customization includes materials like cedar siding set horizontally, bamboo floors, and lots of high-quality aluminum-framed windows.

Other two-bar designs include the Two-Bar L, which Luntz describes as an "elegant and simple crossing of two axes," and which provides 1,790 square feet and three bedrooms; the Two-Bar Slip, which, at 1,740 square feet, has the two bars parallel but joining at their ends to make a common living area and four bedrooms on either end for a perfect large-family or duplex situation; and the Two-Bar Bridge with Sleeping Porch at 1,960 square feet with a bridging bar of two bedrooms on the second floor and a sleeping porch off of a terrace.

Among the three-bar designs is the Three-Bar Bridge with Guest House, the largest of the config-

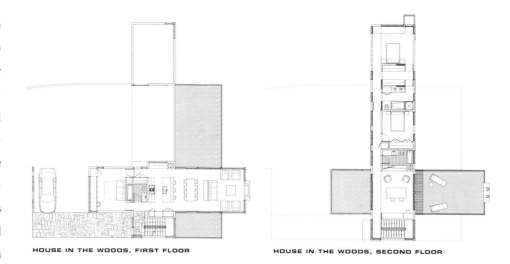

HOUSE IN THE WOODS, FIRST FLOOR   HOUSE IN THE WOODS, SECOND FLOOR

urations, shaped like a "Z" and with 2,660 square feet of floor space.

From this design came Summer Retreat, a home in East Hampton, New York, that includes four bedrooms so it can be easily rented out for the summer. This house was customized down to budget—the owner computed what it could be rented for and that figured directly into the budgeting of the building. The house also includes a media room, a sleeping porch, a six-vehicle carport, and a pool area.

LEFT: House in the Woods was created for a North Carolina couple who didn't have a large amount of money to spend. The houses in the system cost about $125 per square foot, depending on the area of the country. ABOVE: The house is an example of the two-bar system, where public and private spaces cross in separate bars.

SUMMER RETREAT, FIRST FLOOR

SUMMER RETREAT, SECOND FLOOR

Other three-bar designs include the Three-Bar T, which has 1,575 square feet of floor space, four bedrooms, and two courtyards formed by the crossing of the T, and the Three-Bar Bridge with Three-Story Tower, at 2,530 square feet one of the most ambitious of the designs, with a sleeping porch at the top of the tower.

ABOVE and RIGHT: Summer Retreat, which was created for a single man who wanted to rent out the house during summers, is an example of the most complicated of the designs, the Three-Bar Bridge with Guest House. Three bars intersect, creating 2,660 square feet in a "Z" pattern.

Houses designed from the firm's system, the partners say, can be ready about nine months after they are ordered. Tanney estimates that houses from this system cost an average of $125 per square foot, depending on the area of the country in which the house is built and added details such as fireplaces and the like. He compares that to the cost of their stick-built homes, which run about $250 to $400 a square foot. The prices are low, Tanney says, partly because the element of a brand new design is taken out of the process and because every place that square footage can be maximized in the modules, it is. "Because of the smart square footage savings and the savings that we can get from making these modules in a factory, we believe that we can increase the quality of the detailing, that we can increase the quality of the materials," says Tanney.

Tanney and Luntz developed their practice largely by designing Manhattan lofts, which are often deep and narrow, and brought this experience to bear with the modules. Tanney thinks of the homes in the system as "freestanding lofts," with some of the same specific and efficient design approaches such as sculptural built-in furniture, the building of storage space into the walls, and the compact layout of bathrooms and other functional spaces. Many high-quality elements are employed: bathrooms, for instance, are then finished with materials like glass tile; the kitchens may use steel, slate, or limestone and maple cabinets; the interior doors may be frosted glass; the exterior

siding can be cedar. But the firm also saves money by using low-cost materials in imaginative ways, such as corrugated metal or cement board as a hip exterior finishing material, utilitarian light fixtures that bring industrial chic, and fiberboard or recycled sawdust for wall finishes that have a fresh look.

Tanney feels that systems like this will "integrate the architect in with society," enabling people to afford homes designed by architects. He sees the success of approaches like Resolution: 4 Architecture's as a natural evolution from the increased focus on design that can be seen in other forms throughout the country, from firms like Design Within Reach that sell affordable furniture to retailers like Target that are hiring designers and architects to make their products. If we have Banana Republic clothes, the logic goes, shouldn't we have well-designed houses? That's the goal of today's prefab—better design for less money. ∎

michael graves & associates

BRIGHTON PAVILION | HEATHCOTE PAVILION | SHERWOOD PAVILION

The prefab additions to houses that architect Michael Graves has designed for Target are appealing enough that, like a lot of items from the store, shoppers might look for an excuse to take one home. What is remarkable, of course, is that one *can* be taken home, and added onto the home—reminiscent of the historic Sears, Roebuck and Co., houses that were ordered by catalogue and shipped on trains to customers all over the country.

The Graves/Target additions are particularly notable for their high design. A figure of Graves's stature, an icon of contemporary American architecture, known internationally for his work with museums, universities, and public structures as well as private homes, does not usually have his buildings arrive in the backyards of homes across the country. If Graves is available for the work, in fact, he usually charges about $20,000 in design fees alone to add a custom room to a house. Reporting on the development, the *Wall Street Journal* put it this way: "People who could never afford to hire Graves . . . can still crow to the neighbors that he helped design their homes."

Now, in the same store where people pick out their sheets and pick up their laundry detergent, there are three different designs of home additions, which Target calls Pavilions. They range in price from $10,000 to $26,000 for materials and plans; labor and preparation of the site adds another $5,000 to $15,000. The buildings can also stand alone away from houses as studios, offices, potting sheds, yoga rooms, or pool rooms that "continue a tradition of outbuilding as architectural accessories for the home," says Graves. Two of the models especially, Brighton and Heathcote, are distinctive buildings, their own little edifices, with wall and roof designs that evoke the kind of structures that used to be found in town squares and public parks. The Brighton is an octagon, with the option of walls or windows or a combination of both along the eight sides. With walls, it can be a library; with all windows, it is instantly an artist's studio, sunroom, or breakfast room with panoramic views. The

RIGHT: The Brighton is one of the three structures that Michael Graves has designed for Target. The structures can be freestanding or attached to houses to add rooms and can be bought online. Models of them will be appearing at some Targets to give people an idea of their size and scale.

Heathcote has walk-in niches on the sides for tucking furniture into, perhaps for a library, media room, home office, or game room. All of the pavilions are larger than they appear in phtographs, with 13-foot ceilings and an equal amount of width and depth.

When customers log onto Target's website, they can indulge a fantasy of 33 different combinations based on the three designs—changing siding, color palettes, and details like screening or curtains for the open-air model, the Sherwood. This outdoor room has a rustic crisscross of beams at the top and for flooring offers a continuation of the ground around it, be it grass, wildflowers, or cedar chips, or a concrete slab for a more structured space. It can be used as a porch, poolhouse, a place for outdoor entertaining, or a spot for gardening implements and gathering flowers, drying herbs, or storing baskets of vegetables.

In sketches that look like blueprints and evolve into photograph-like animation as the buildings take shape, the website takes customers through the steps of choosing one of the three models, deciding whether it is to be attached or unattached from the house, finding a color that is appropriate (with roof colors that change with siding colors, such as white with a blue roof, ivory with a green one, and shadow green with a gray one), and siding materials including tongue and groove, a garden wall for growing vegetation on the outside, and glass, screening, or curtains depending on the model. After the information is e-mailed in, Lindal Cedar Homes, which handles the actual building of the structures through their distributors across the country, contacts the customer and does a site visit, goes over building codes, and initiates the other procedures that go into the building.

It is the ease of expansion to the home that is the biggest selling point of the Pavilions. Compared to the usual process of renovation, which Graves calls "cumbersome, costly, and disruptive," they are fast, clean, and simple. Because of the way the Pavilions are designed, most houses only need lose a door or window to add one on, rather than an entire wall or wing. Lindal Cedar Homes provides the builder and contractors through their distributors, so there is a built-in trust factor with a proven company. And the Pavilions can go up in as few as 50 hours (a few take as many as 200 hours), depending on the site, house, and model chosen. With a three-person crew, it could take as little as a week to add a room onto a home.

In addition to eliminating the old equation between home expansion and choking on sawdust, the Pavilions add a touch of sophistication to the American landscape. Because they can be customized with colors and materials that are designed to adjust to different regions, climates, and architectural styles, they fit in with all kinds of homes, "enhancing the house instead of matching it, like a piece of jewelry," says Jeff Caden of Lindal Cedar Homes.

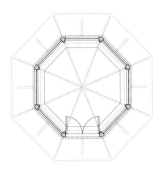
BRIGHTON PAVILION

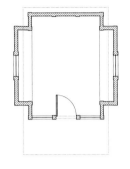
HEATHCOTE PAVILION

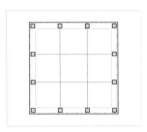
SHERWOOD PAVILION

Though Graves has no definite plans to create a full-scale prefab house, the Pavilions would certainly be a precursor, and Gary Lapera of Graves's office admits that they are "a kind of microcosm of the issues you'd run into trying to produce mass housing." In the meantime, people can get used to the rather radical idea of having these stunning little buildings, at the click of a mouse, join their own homes and become part of them. ▪

TOP LEFT: The Heathcote is full of details like a round window, a window wall in the front, and a charmingly shaped roof. BOTTOM LEFT: The Sherwood is intended for outdoor use, with the option of glass, screening, or curtains. ABOVE: The Pavilions are designed to be distinctive, octagonally shaped like the Brighton or with niches like the Heathcote. When combining them with different siding and color options, there are 33 possible combinations, all visible on the Internet.

su11 architecture + design

The stereotype about prefab is that it creates cookie-cutter homes and limits the choices of homeowners. What is true, however, and increasingly so, is that prefab allows more creativity and individualism, not less. Su11, a New York architecture and design firm whose principals, Ferda Kolatan and Erich Schoenenberger, are both of European origin, is proposing an amazing opportunity for homeowners to realize their own homes, piece by piece, with a completely original idea called the Composite Housing project.

The project begins with a skeleton of a house formed from a variety of shapes to make whatever size or dimension of home is desired. The skeleton would be built by a local contractor from wood or steel. The house would then be personally designed by each homeowner with "add-ons," innovative units that are a combination of appliances and furniture, walls, ceil-

LEFT: The Composite Housing Project starts with a skeleton and has different-colored "add-ons" that shape an individual house and have different functions. The add-ons put all the functional elements together in compact spaces, allowing the rest of the house to be used as flexible living space.

ings, and floors, and other architectural elements. They are pieces of houses put together in ways that are normally never thought of, and so allow a new perspective on how to design a house, and therefore, new kinds of houses. For example, one add-on is an entrance door combined with a staircase to the roof and also with a basement, all in one unit. Another is an entrance door with a cabinet and a storage room on the inside of the house and a shower on the exterior. This idea of combining indoor and outdoor architecture in one unit extends to things like an indoor fireplace combined with stairs and an outdoor barbecue grill. A kitchen unit (with appliances to be fit into the unit later) also has stairs to the terrace, a terrace canopy, and a storage room. A bathroom unit (also with fittings to be added later) is combined with outdoor wood storage.

The outside surface of the add-ons is made of epoxy so they can be used both indoors and out, and because it is easy to maintain, ages well, and just as important, comes in an almost infinite variety of colors. The colors offered in this arrangement are truly inspiring, bringing life and art into the home; they promote the idea of embracing color and not being afraid of it, as has so often been true of home design. They are bright and bold and happy. The homeowner

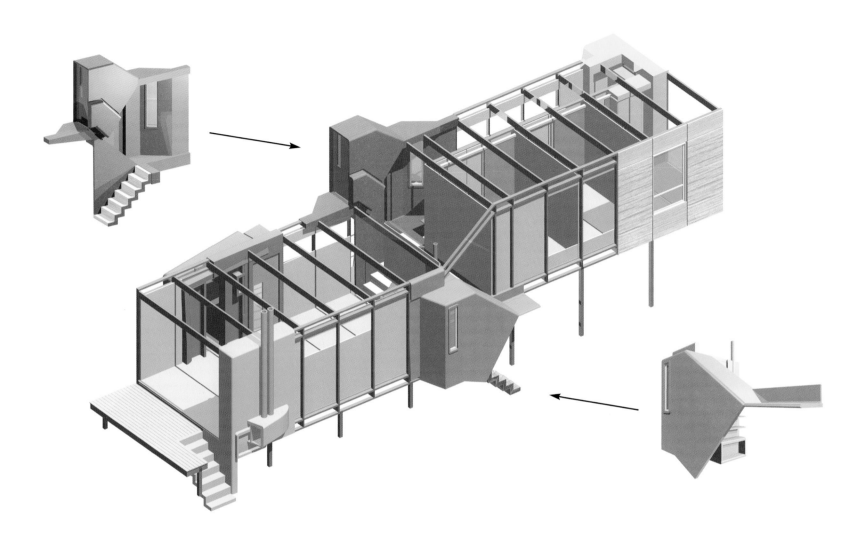

chooses the color for each unit, so many different colors may be used in one house, creating a real vibrancy. This use of color is itself a major change in the nature of home design.

What the add-ons do for a house is to put all the functional elements together in compact spaces, allowing the rest of the house to be used as flexible living space, however people want to use it. At the same time, the add-ons are aesthetically interesting: they don't try to conceal the functional nature of elements like stairs and storage spaces but rather celebrate them. In other words, they get the functional elements out of the way, in a sense, to make space for living, but out of the way in a manner that is unique

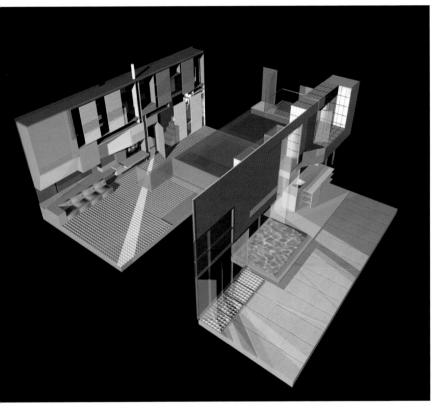

and extremely visually appealing, adding significantly to the overall design quality and character of the house. Because of their saturated color and sculptural design, the add-ons largely define the aesthetic of the home.

Kolatan and Schoenenberger like to think that they would be selling not just houses but ideas. Their program brings it all back to the question of "What is a house?"—one that homeowners can ask and answer for themselves.

The add-ons give almost limitless possibilities and a design freedom to homeowners that is not com-

mon today, opening up consideration of where rooms are located in houses and how one space relates to another. The add-ons can also encourage new thoughts about design because of how they are structured. For the appliance sections of the house, for example, they are configured in space units. So one unit (in space terms) allows room for a toilet, two for a sink cabinet, three for a shower, and four for a bathtub. It helps to be able to think in those quantifiable terms, because a homeowner can assess possibilities more easily and therefore think more freely about how to design. The add-ons are like big Legos, and one can make virtually whatever one wants out of them. "We always take Legos as a compliment," says Kolatan.

This concept is the ultimate in prefab—the add-ons would be sold by catalog and the Internet, with the customer having choices of color, type, and size. They would then be manufactured and delivered to the site to be installed. Add-ons would be constantly updated to reflect taste and industry improvement, and people would be able to exchange their old ones for new ones when they had a change in preference.

Kolatan and Schoenenberger think this is an idea that is in tune with the times because our culture is now full of so many choices and puts a big premium on individual vision and freedom. Systems in general are becoming less fixed and more fluid, so homes should reflect that. This belief is evident in their Composite Architecture, a different set of add-ons that combine furniture and architecture, "putting a variety of different functions onto one continuous shape," says Schoenenberger. Laminated surfaces change color or texture (all of which are custom chosen from many patterns and colors) to show the change of function within the unit. So one piece combines a sofa and desk to facilitate the frequent transitions people make today between work and leisure: another a table and storage; another a sound system and shelving to create a library.

The idea, says su11, is for people to be able to program their homes the way they program com-

puters. The company's website will feature an interactive animation through which the users can click on an add-on unit and change it—first with a shelf, then a shelf and a bench, then with the bench changing into a sink, for example—to see all the different possibilities and choose one. They will also be able to choose from a range of materials and colors, take a virtual tour of the house they create, and see "montages" of different add-ons put together.

In the same spirit, su11 created the + System, which doesn't include add-ons but does achieve a similar result by putting all the functional elements—baths, storage, kitchen—in what they call "shelves" on either side of the structure. These shelving units—just nine-by-three-by-eight-foot structures—allow the area in the center to be used for living space. Both freedom and structure are given to the living area as it sits between the shelving units on either side. Anything can be put in the shelving in any order, according to each homeowner's needs. "It can be many different houses following a similar principle," says Kolatan. ▪

LEFT and RIGHT: The + System has two disctinct zones. The "shelves" house the functional elements of the house, like bathrooms, storage, stairs, and appliances. The "Flex-Space" is an open zone; the shelves sit on either side of it. This space is intended for activities like sleeping, working, playing, relaxing, partying, cooking, dining, and the like.

CHAPTER 3

the **future** of prefab

homes on the **cutting edge**

New prefab projects are turning up all the time. Like a field of flowers in the spring, the landscape of prefab is changing almost every day, so it can be hard to keep up with. Here is a collection of some promising new projects, many still in the planning stage, some about to or already taking off. Because they are so new, some of the details and specifications may change. But they give some sense of what there is to explore and to dream about for those looking for prefab.

Alchemy Architecture

The weeHouse is true to its name, a structure that contains no more than the space one needs, a refreshing idea in this age of senselessly rambling houses. The first house, which the firm refers to as "little prefab on the prairie" in reference to its site, was made for just the sort of person today's prefab helps—a Minnesota orchestra violinist

Alchemy Architecture: weeHouse

with a two-year-old son—someone who doesn't earn a huge income but nonetheless loves good design.

The functional but distinctly charming space was brought in whole on a truck and craned onto the site. It is made of a standard wood-and-steel frame with an exterior of oxidized metal. Full-height, full-width sliding glass doors let light into the space. The interior is made of fir and features a wood stove and fixtures and furnishings from Ikea, an appropriate choice for a well-designed but inexpensive house. The house cost a total of only $45,000.

Edgar Blazona

The glowing boxes that make up the Modular Dwelling series are, with their spare forms and translucent front walls, radical in their simplicity. Made of four walls and usually consisting of one room, some models are portable and all are easy to transport and assemble. They address the requirements of living space at their most basic level. Yet the design is elegant, based on the examples of Charles Eames and Richard Neutra and built with the care and detailing of high-quality furniture. Indeed, Blazona is also a furniture designer and welder. He says that for him, designing a house is like "making a big giant cabinet. It's just like shipping an armoire, but you need a forklift or a crane." Prefabrication of a house is like furniture—as Blazona points out, you can control the outcome on a machine or in an indoor space much more than you can in the field, building in the traditional way.

Of the three models that currently exist, two are portable, one built as a guest room and another as a dwelling at 2003's Burning

Edgar Blazona: Modular Dwelling

areas of design for inspiration, and use computers in innovative ways to achieve their goals.

The Slide-Rule House brings all of these elements together. It is designed in modules by floor, so that the first and second stories can be arranged in different relationships with one another once the modules arrive onsite. The structure of the house is standard wood framing; a steel-frame model is also available. With the wood frame, there is a choice of the house being assembled onsite or premanufactured. There is also a choice of metal finishes and window types. Each module has built-in rails and niches that mark different possible areas for windows. As the Slide-Rule demonstrates, the more flexible the design process, the more options the finished product will have. Customizing the house yet keeping it simple and affordable helps realize the firm's dream of bringing architecture and popular culture closer together.

All materials are easy to access anywhere, and contractors can put together the house simply. It is 1,686 square feet and takes about eight weeks to be delivered.

Man festival, a counterculture celebration held in the Nevada desert every year. This accessibility to a nonconventional home owning audience—the ability to "purchase modernism, bring it to your backyard," as Blazona puts it—speaks to the socialist aspect of today's prefab, where individuality is a critical element.

These structures are an "artform" to Blazona, as well. One model features awnings that extend out from a window wall with such expression that they are practically a sculptural detail—yet still completely functional. Using industrial materials, even the large models with many elements cost less than $500,000. They are furnished with original designs and vintage modernist pieces.

Choi-Campagna Design

Choi-Campagna is known for their use of unconventional materials from other industries like transportation. They also look to other

Choi-Campagna Design: Slide-Rule House

Jones, Partners: Architecture

The Jones, Partners' Program Container System (PRO/con) uses recycled shipping containers in an innovative way. Twenty-foot containers as units can be leased or bought by homeowners and outfitted as distinct spaces such as a kitchen, home office, closet, and so forth. In between the containers, panels form what the firm calls "free space," glass-walled areas that vary the look of the structure and provide for more customized rooms that can be used as the owner wishes. The 8-by-20-foot panels form the floors, walls, ceilings, and roofs, and, in an efficient approach, can be shipped in the containers that will make up the rest of the house.

The floor panels are made of recycled wood, the roof panels are solar to provide heating and cooling for the house, and the containers themselves are a recycled element, so there are several environmental advantages.

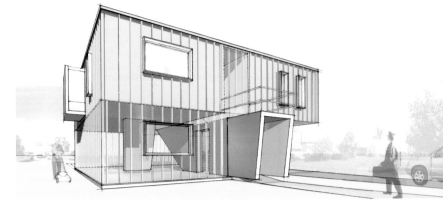

Lewis.Tsurumaki.Lewis: Upside House

The highly customizable system allows for many different configurations upon assembly. The innovation of the plan comes from the fact that factory-prepared elements (the outfitted containers) are combined with a panel system that is prepared on site and can be changed again and again as the needs of the homeowners change. Wes Jones says, "It does not view the house as finished product but as a continuously negotiated collection of products and their ultimate relation to the ever-changing American family."

Lewis.Tsurumaki.Lewis

Upside House has been designed by Lewis.Tsuramaki.Lewis to fit the dimensions of the standard developer lot while maintaining the sense of open space central to so much modern design. The first floor is one single space and the second is a block of bedrooms. From the second to the first story hang architectural components for functional purposes, such as powder rooms, media walls, hearths, and aquariums. It is this landscape of components (called "drop-ins" and "cut-ups" by the architects) and how they are used and arranged differently for each house that make it both customizable and aesthetically distinctive.

Jones, Partners: Architecture: Program Container System (PRO/con)

The two floors are connected by the "core," which contains essential elements of surburban life like the mailbox, porch, front door, central staircase, kitchen, skylight, balcony, barbecue grill, and the like. The house is wrapped in translucent polycarbonate material so that sunlight can enter from every angle during the day; at night the interior of the lit house is visible, as Paul Lewis puts it, like "an X ray." Windows can be put wherever desired along this translucent material that wraps around the house.

Although the standard model is 2,094 square feet, the house is also customized according to the amount of space needed. As rooms need to be added the house can extend back on the lot. As it does, the stairwell changes, becoming more subtly sloped and "gracious," as the firm describes it.

The framing is standard and the delivery time for the house is about eight weeks. The triumph of this house is that as its functions change, its aesthetics do too, in more interesting ways than a standard design would allow.

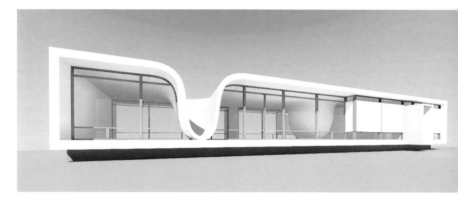

William Massie: House from the Architecture Gallery

LOT-EK

LOT-EK is a firm that takes industrial materials all sorts of places outside their traditional realm. They refer to their Container Kit as a "product." This new, straightforward approach is part of the changing way we look at homes—as something that can be made and ordered, like items from a houseware catalogue. The kit takes the simplest possible approach to house design, using a shipping container and breaking the home down into basic elements like closet, counter, bed, and bathtub.

Their Guzman Penthouse, produced for a private client in New York City, solves the problem of space limitations in the dense metropolis. The structure is a simple translucent box with a terrace built onto the end, all framed by a container. Prefabrication allowed for the addition to be planned and made before it reached the confined area of the rooftop where it would finally reside.

William Massie

William Massie's Architecture Gallery—a selection of house systems—is, like much today in prefab, revolutionary. The houses made under this system are designed, customized, and blueprinted on a computer

LOT-EK: Container Kit

that then directly programs machines to create the pieces of the house. The factory-assembled structure is then shipped to the house's site. The pieces are made of "R-control" panels, preinsulated panels with a 32 insulation rating that come complete with installed rough electrical and plumbing. They are then sprayed with a high-density, low-maintenance plastic customarily used for truck bed liners. As such, they are resistant to temperature changes and the regular expansion and contraction of most materials used in housing. The colors of this plastic are also bright and varied, making for bold houses.

In addition to addressing the owner's sense of style, computers also customize the house according to the site conditions such as solar gain, wind exposure, and other physical characteristics. Upon purchasing a house, a team from the firm will site the house, work with a local contractor to build the foundation, arrange for a local plumber and electrician, and secure local building approval. The system has a number of different designs in varying sizes and, wonderfully, colors. As Massie says, prefabrication in this case "makes the extraordinary possible at an ordinary price."

mk architecture

Michelle Kaufmann created the Glidehouse because she, her husband, and their dog needed what so many are looking for today—a well-designed but affordable home that is also ecologically sensitive and easy to maintain. The Glidehouse gets its name from the design, which aims to cut down on clutter and focus on the feeling of living clean and simply. Storage for everything from media and books to clothing and cooking is put in a bar on one side of the house; gliding wood panels can be placed in front of the storage space for the look of a simple wood wall. The opposite side of the house also has gliding panels, but they are made of glass, with clerestory windows above them to create breezes through the house and facilitate contact with the outdoors.

Since the house is designed, as Kaufmann puts it, to "collaborate with nature," it is also "green." Indirect lighting from the glassy design minimizes the need for electric lighting during the day and solar panels and a wind generator make it possible for the house to run on its own, without being connected to electricity lines. This brings the long-term cost down and also means that the house can be placed just

mk archtecture: Glidehouse

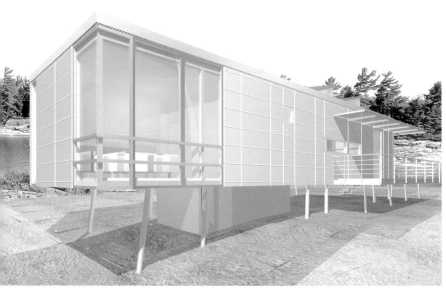

Nottoscale: Modulome

about anywhere. The exterior walls are made of cor-ten steel, a maintenance-free metal. It is built to the highest codes for weather resistance.

The house can be shipped anywhere in the United States or Canada, arriving as two or three truckloads of prefabricated parts, depending on whether there are two or three bedrooms in the house. The cost is about $110 a square foot.

Nottoscale

The Modulome system uses approaches from the automobile industry for residential design. The core of the system is a structural steel chassis, 16 by 48 by 10 feet. The chassis has predrilled holes that all other elements of the building attach to with bolts. The chassis is trucked to the site completely assembled, where it is placed on columns that are specific to the site. This frame then becomes the basis on which all other elements are placed—flooring, roof, and panels that make the exterior walls. These panels come in different widths to accommodate different functions. The other building units, such as the kitchen and bathroom, can be placed anywhere within the frame of the chassis, allowing for what might be the ultimate customization—different layouts with different amounts of space within the same frame.

The customization continues into the future, as well, as people live and change with their space. Since none of the panels or other building elements are permanently attached, they can be changed as the needs of the owner evolve. Elements such as a breakfast nook, a wall of sliding doors, or a carport can also be added.

pH Architects

David Pysh and Alex Hurst describe their Suburban Loft as "a design intended to provide the inhabitants with the opportunity for exploration, intimacy, comfort, and dreams," which is much more than most houses of any kind can offer. The house is notably different from most standard layouts, with the main area of circulation put on one

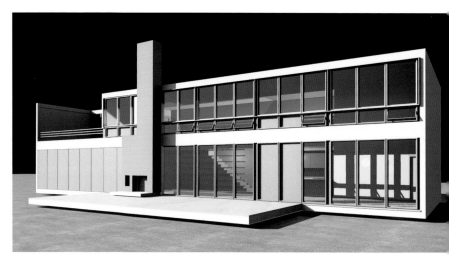

pH Architects: Suburban Loft

Alastair Reilly: Drumpoint Experimental House

side, rather than in the center, of the home, and the plumbing system placed in the center as a wall that divides the public and private areas. This economy of design allows space for an expansive, 16-foot-high living and dining area.

Standard materials and building techniques are used to make the house accessible to almost any area of the country, but the construction is well detailed and the design is highly customized according to site and owner's preferences. Pysh and Hurst are aiming here to "create grandeur in the design for the common home, which is both reserved and inspiring, comfortable yet elegant."

Alastair Reilly

The Drumpoint Experimental House, a prototype that is set near the Chesapeake Bay, is constructed from commercial materials used in innovative ways. Light-gauge steel, insulated panels, and a stucco finish make up the house. The 8-by-20-foot wall panels can also form interior walls, and vertical translucent panels have spots that let in pure light, making the small spaces of the house seem larger

and bringing the outdoor environment inside. Each 4-by-8-foot module built from the panels can be easily transported by truck to virtually any location.

The resulting 2,000-square-foot house feels much larger than its size would indicate, with spacious no-walled areas that keep the house free to be what it wants to be.

White on White Design

White on White Design has created a small yet comfortable miracle, the $30,000 house, complete with high-design furniture included in the cost. The house is assembled from interchangeable 6-by-12-by-8-foot modules, which can be put together in varying ways to create different design results. Four modules configured and formed together make this house, for a total of 576 square feet. Inspired by all kinds of glass houses, from Philip Johnson's to Craig Ellwood's, the house is so affordable and also so aesthetically pleasing precisely because of its simplicity. It's a gem.

The one-bedroom home features a built-in bed, a glass skylight, a well-applianced kitchen, a dining table and six chairs, a sofa, two of the company's typically International Style "Barclelona"

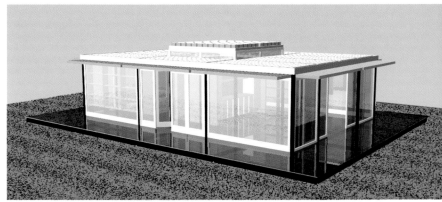

White on White Design: $30,000 House

chairs, and a built-in bench. With this house, White on White Design look to be fulfilling the motto that pops up on their website: "Bringing Design to the Masses."

Blake Williams

Published as part of the Seattle Case Study Homes Program of 2002 (on which Williams has also written a book), Colin is a uniquely thoughtful project. From the outside, the stainless steel finish reflects the landscape and sky, making it perfect for a setting in nature. By day, the house allows a number of views, and by night, the more private areas have less exposure for more comfort. The floors on the first level are shiny blue integral-color concrete, while the upper level is plywood for floors, walls, and ceilings. Wood-fiber cabinetry sits on casters so that it can be rearranged for all different designs.

The "green" elements include a photovoltaic roof system that powers the house, an electric toilet that allows the owner to bypass the local system, and a basin that collects dew and rainwater for the garden. The two-bedroom house comes in two module pieces, with 750 square feet on the first floor and 800 on the second floor.

Sources for New Designs

As prefab brings almost daily surprises in terms of who is taking it on and how, information sources and entire businesses have emerged to help homeowners find their ideal prefab homes.

fabprefab.com is an exceptionally useful website that tracks new developments in prefab, updating at least monthly and sometimes sooner the new projects out there that can be hard to track down. The site is well designed and organized, and includes all kinds of other resources like news in the prefab field and links to related resources.

Blake Williams: Colin

etekt.com is not dedicated solely to prefab, but is including more and more prefab projects. The site allows people to see well-designed, reasonably priced projects from some of the finest smaller architects and designers. Bruce Fisher, one of the founders, describes it as "potentially the world's biggest architecture studio." Visiting the site is like looking through a gallery full of treasures.

Modern Modular (modern-modular.com) represents architects who have prefab projects, so that the potential homeowner can go through one source for all their concerns. Principal Peter LaBonte describes it as a "co-op for architects," where their work, for example, can be put together to be produced in one factory for lower costs that are passed on to those buying the houses. LaBonte calls the projects "off the rack" with some customization. Treating prefab like a retail product on the business end makes sense, because that is what the prefab house has become—an item that can be purchased with the ease and the range of choice of any other. ▪

CHAPTER 4

constructing prefab

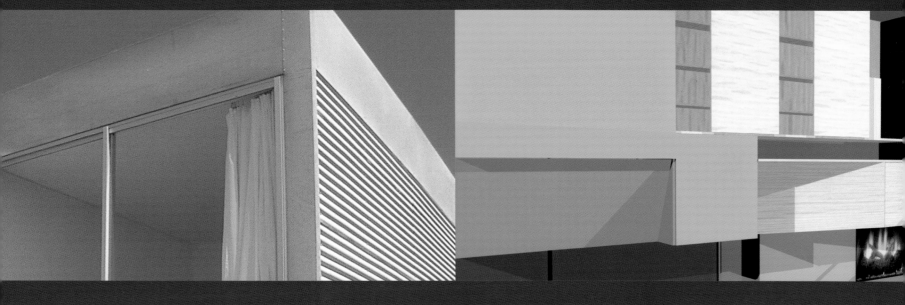

new materials & processes

Prefab buildings are remarkable not just for how they are made but for what they are made of. The materials are innovative, or standard materials used in an innovative way, usually created or chosen with a mind toward getting them to the site. And when innovation and creativity are introduced for one reason, they are usually continued for others. So these materials are often also cost-effective, "green" (ecologically sound), and energy efficient. Today is a whole new world in which to create buildings.

framing

SHIPPING CONTAINERS

Shipping containers made of aluminum or steel and constructed for holding everything from grain to cars are now being enthusiastically used to create homes. The website fabprefab.com passes on a quote that refers to them as "icons of globalization," since they may have traveled the world before ending up in a homeowner's backyard, or right in front of that backyard, as a home. Architect Adam Kalkin refers to their "maritime romance." But it is architect Jennifer Siegal that sums up their latest meaning, calling them "the building blocks of the construction industry." Plentiful and easy to find, inexpensive, and readily adaptable to whatever is being built, they are probably the most popular prefab components today.

Containers can be thought of as modular elements ready to be personalized with each use. They can be used with any number of other materials to suit each home, as Siegal did in combining them with glass to create the Seatrain House in California. The containers can be joined together to create a large area, or stacked for more than one story, or one can be used for a room, or they can be carved up to create pieces of a house.

Because containers were designed to be shipped, they are ideal for transporting. As they were in their former lives, they can be conveyed by truck, ship, or train. They are stronger than homes made from standard materials, standing up to tornadoes, hurricanes, and earthquakes. They are also resistant to water. They were strongly and often lovingly built—some have floors made of mahogany and other woods from the tropics.

Containers are highly cost-effective in terms of the square footage they provide to the structure of a house. They have an industrial chic that is enhanced by the patina of their rust or by the large letters on their sides or by the pulls and rivets that are part of their construction. They can easily be painted, as well, to give them another kind of look.

Siegal's prototype for a hip mobile home, Portable House, is made from a shipping container, and Kalkin's Quik Build House, an owner-assembled prefab priced at under $60,000, is constructed from containers. A model of Kalkin's house is placed right in the shipping container at the manufacturer's yard in New Jersey by the company that provides the containers for the houses. Kalkin says that the company makes whatever modifications are necessary to the containers and ships them out in pieces made to be assembled onsite. In cases where the containers are sent out whole, they still transport easily, since—designed to fit onboard ships—they are modular to start.

Shipping Containers: Jennifer Siegal's Portable House

Containers come in all kinds of sizes and types, and there are several companies in the United States that sell them (a list of these and many other distributors of materials discussed in this chapter appears in the Sources section). Because there are many different types of containers, and they have been made differently throughout the years, customers can consider a variety. One company, ISO Containers, has a "container locator" online, where customers can survey the inventory, which is updated on a regular basis electronically. Containers—available new, used, and modified—come in 20-foot lengths and 40-foot lengths (the latter not made since the 1970s); in "high cube" format, taller than standard; in insulated versions and refrigerated versions; and in a variety of different colors. Interport Maintenance Company will create custom containers and paint and refurbish them. Sea Box, a container company in New Jersey, uses CAD computer tools to computerize the design and execution of the specific building. "Fax us your

specifications or drawings!" they exclaim on their website. By filling out their customer profile, customers will receive a free model of a 20-foot container that can be easily assembled. Allied Container Products promises to configure the containers so that they meet national codes and standards, which can be an important consideration, depending upon in what part of the country the house will be built. None of these companies are used to getting many orders yet for houses, as they traditionally draw their customers from the industrial arena, but they are accommodating and are beginning to see the advantages of the trend.

The next frontier in making homes from former transportation vehicles may be old railroad cars; as with containers, there are many all across the country and they were also made to travel. They can be made into many different configurations the way shipping containers can, though they are smaller; together, the two kinds of structures allow for a wide variety of designs.

Steel Structures: Rick Wintersole's Garret Residence

STEEL STRUCTURES

Butler Buildings, available from Butler Steel, are similar to shipping containers, but they are made new and are more pared down in design. Available in many different sizes (40 by 50 feet, 30 by 100 feet, 33 by 40 feet, and so on), they have similar properties to shipping containers, perhaps without the mystique but with a cleaner, fresher feel. Many houses, particularly mobile ones, are now built with aluminum frames from sources found by the architects, often of recyclable grade.

Steel frames that are usually employed for industrial structures are beginning to be used in residential ones. Classic Steel Homes in Houston designs frames for homes by simply feeding the design into their computer, which then directs how the metal is bent, shaped, and cut into the custom design. All steel pieces are sent to the site, down to the screws, and the frame is assembled within a few days.

Looking like beams in an industrial barn, the steel can be visible within the house. Rick Wintersole, the architect on these projects, prefers this, wondering why something as wonderful as the look of steel beams crisscrossing one another at the ceiling would be covered up. He also admires the adaptability of the material, and has built an upright urban-looking house as well as a rambling suburban house with this sort of frame. "It doesn't have to look like an airstreamed trailer," says Wintersole. In one of Wintersole's houses, he used steel materials like stairs, fixtures, and shelves to finish the structure and celebrate the material across the house.

PANELS

Panelized construction has been used in making prefab homes for years. Now architects are taking that system and using it for high design, in visionary and individual houses, and with better and more interesting materials. With panelization, the house, and particularly the framing, is literally made of panels. This system may remind one of a gingerbread house, with each piece having its place in making the structure. Panels are made indoors and installed onsite, often with numbers to identify each panel and where it goes. Windows and doors are often already planned for in different panels; some panel systems have electrical and plumbing systems already installed in them. Advances in panelization allow for architects to create unique houses from a system—they can be constructed in a factory, yet still allow for a seemingly infinite variety of designs.

Structural insulated panels (SIPs) are being used by Anderson Anderson Architecture to create custom houses. The sandwich panels have a Styrofoam-insulated core with plywood or particle board on either side. They can be made in whatever shape and size is needed for the particular character of the house. Anderson Anderson often adds birchwood, veneer, or any number of other high-end materials to finish the panels and individualize the house.

Architects like William Massie are experimenting with making their own materials for prefab houses. His involve Styrofoam panels sprayed with concrete; these are created by a computer that programs how each panel will be shaped for use in the house. Other architects are using panels made of more traditional materals used in unusual ways. Architect David Hertz's Tilt-Up Slab House in Venice, California, was made from 14 concrete panels, the majority of which were poured offsite and trucked in to be connected to the steel that helps support the house. The interior side of the panels was left exposed and became the inside walls of the house after being sanded, sealed, and waxed to continue the simple elegance of the concrete exterior. The floors are burnished concrete, which are radiant heated from the solar panels of the roof. Even the showers and tubs have a white cement-plaster finish to continue the look.

With in-laws in the refrigeration business, Hertz has also used refrigeration panels to build. Hertz considered how meat lockers work and talked to ice house manufacturers to prepare for building. The resulting structure is solid, and the 4-by-15-foot panels, which are made of six inches of foam with metal on either side, are easily put together with clips and levers. The panels are resistant to fire and weather, and are incredibly energy efficient; no air-conditioning or heating is needed. "The interior temperature will be consistently different from the exterior temperature," says Hertz, because of the fact that these panels go to the opposite extreme in either type of climate, cold or hot.

Architect Steven Holl used 30 metal panels to build the Turbulence House, each with a unique shape and none more than eight feet wide so that they would fit into a container to be shipped. The panels, which are aluminum, were digitally made from Holl's design, then put together onsite on a remote mesa in New Mexico. Computers make possible this kind of design involving odd-shaped metal panels.

exterior finishes

Holl's metal house was finished with Galvalume, a popular material for prefab today that was also used by architect Rocio Romero for her LV House. The light-colored finish is made of galvanized tin that has been coated with aluminum. Zincalume is a similar material, made of steel that has been covered in aluminum and zinc alloy. Architects Collins and Turner have used recycled-grade aluminum and anodized aluminum for their Lantern model.

Architects are also finding new and unexpected uses for more conventional materials. Resolution: 4 Architecture uses corrugated metal, cement board, and cedar siding placed horizontally for their exteriors. Using standard materials means that a design may be

Exterior Finishes: Rocio Romero's LV House

built anywhere in the country, which is the point of prefab, of course. If a manufacturer supplies the same material in Texas as it does in Los Angeles, it can be used for a prefab house in any place. So Anderson Anderson Architecture, for example, wrapped a house they designed in two colors of standard asphalt roll roofing, creating a siding that is inexpensive, colorful, and fire resistant. The material is common; it is its innovative use that is key to intelligent design and to a creative aesthetic.

For the actual roof of the house, however, Anderson Anderson used corrugated galvanized steel roofing. Metal roofs, which are also fireproof, are being used extensively in prefab houses for their convenience and sleek looks. They are widely available in a huge array of styles and colors.

interiors

The interiors of prefab houses can be just as interesting as the exteriors. Floors are often made of concrete or Plyboo, a new bamboo product; walls are made of glass; and ceilings of highly finished tongue-and-groove wood that is usually reserved for more public features like the exteriors of houses.

Concrete floors and even walls are used today—they are often radiant heated and therefore highly energy efficient, absorbing the rays of the sun and retaining their heat. Burnished concrete makes for slightly smoother, more elegant-looking concrete floors. "Self-finishing" materials, as architect Huw Turner calls them, such as concrete, stainless steel, and glass, are perfect for prefab.

Plyboo, the latest trend in flooring, is cut and planed from whole timber-sized bamboo, laminated together, and finished, like plywood flooring made from hardwood. Bamboo planks that are finished are also used in flooring. Because bamboo grows extremely fast

and no trees are cut down when it is used, it is an ecologically sound choice. Part of its allure as a prefab material is that it is lightweight, so it is easier to transport than hardwoods. It is also superior in density and durability, and at $5 to $7 a square foot, costs less than hardwood. Bamboo is surprisingly strong—stronger than steel in tension and concrete in compression.

Bamboo, no longer considered a "poor man's timber," is seen today as chic and appreciated for its lovely amber color. Walls, floors, and baseboards are being made from its different forms. In addition to Plyboo, these include scraps of bamboo that are molded together for a solid surface and "floating" bamboo floors that have a veneer of prefinished bamboo over a foundation of compressed fiberboard. Jennifer Siegal uses bamboo materials in her Portable House, an excellent example of its versatility.

Siegal, who researched "smart materials" during a fellowship at Harvard University, has introduced a number of ecologically sound and affordable materials to the prefab world that are also kinetic and lightweight. She has created "woven walls," with wood twining among steel supports; walls of recycled newspaper; and an Ecology Sun System, which uses glass panels with aluminum louvers to filter sunlight from curtain walls to control solar heat gain.

As prefab designs become increasingly high-end, the materials have also gotten immeasurably better. Many use wool carpet, mosaic tile, and birch cabinetry. Stylish glass screens divide the rooms of several of these houses, and stainless steel, black steel, and other sleek materials appear in the kitchens. Fixtures are beautifully designed. Elegant new materials have been invented, like the fiberboard made from recycled sawdust by Resolution: 4 Architecture or the compressed strawboard ceiling paneling made by Collins and Turner. Anderson Anderson Architecture has found a way to make standard materials urbane and fun. They have taken double-hung aluminum windows, joined them together in threes, and turned them sideways so that a picture window is created from standard windows. All of these innovations take advantage of the cost efficiency of prefab, either in building (from the prefab nature of the structure itself) so that the high-end materials can be used, or in the relative inexpensiveness of the materials themselves. This is the result of having architects involved in the creation of prefab: the innovation creates savings and good design at the same time. The savings can then be passed on to make the house even better designed.

built-in and molded designs

Part of what is making prefab houses work today are molded or built-in designs that save space and can be created offsite and brought to the house. Tim Pyne's m-house uses built-in beds and cabinets; Resolution: 4 Architecture has sculptural chairs and other parts of the furniture plan blending with the walls in its bar-system houses.

Molded designs can take advantage of new materials such as Syndecrete, a lightweight concrete made with recycled objects like glass, wood chips, and electronic parts. A solid-surfacing material, it can be ground, polished, or textured in the tradition of terrazzo. Stairways, fireplaces, hip-looking bathtubs, kitchen counters, and even flooring have been made from it in a variety of colors. It can be used almost anywhere, since it is heat retardant, has great thermal and acoustic properties, and is resistant to water, staining, corrosion, and impact damage.

In a very different way, su11 Architects have created something similar with their Composite Housing system. These pieces of houses may have walls, stairways, doors, terraces, or appliances attached to them. The "add-ons" that make up the system are cov-

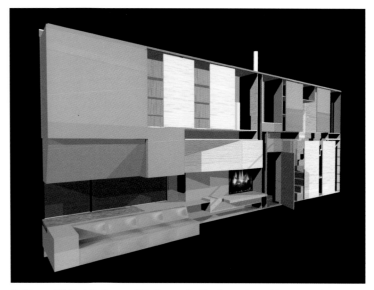

Built-in and Molded Designs: su11's Composite Housing system add-ons

ered in epoxy, which allows a range of colors and makes them usable indoors or out. Inside the houses, the firm uses high-quality laminates and vinyls. (For more, see the section on su11 in the Profiles chapter of the book.)

Other architects are beginning to experiment with the idea of molding parts of houses to make them in a different way. Sultan Kolatan of KOL/MAC Studio is using materials from auto bodywork to make components for houses. These include Bond-O, which works with foam to create shapes, and 3-D optical glass from car technology. Like fiberglass, she says, these materials don't have a scale, as traditional brick does, for example, so they introduce a new dimension to house design.

Materials will continue to be developed and used in different ways as prefab continues to become more central to the vernacular of housing design. ▪

building guidelines

Of course, prefab homes are partly designed to make everything easier. Here are some general guidelines and questions you should address in order to make sure things go smoothly, with the best and most economical results, as you bring your prefab house from concept to realization.

land

Choosing the right piece of property may be the most important part of the process. Of course, you want a place you love, but there are other considerations that will inevitably affect both your comfort and the final cost and value of the home. Here are some major factors:

Building codes and permits: Find out everything you can about the local and regional building codes, permit processes, and the like. Be sure you will be able to do what you want to do with your home, and that prefab is not a problem. Prefab houses are more and more common and the trend will only continue to grow, but you may still encounter some obstacles and prejudices.

Site preparation costs: Preparing the site can be pretty simple or it can literally double the costs of your home. Determine what will be required for utilities such as phone, gas, and electric lines to reach your site. Will you require a septic tank? Do you need a filtering system? If you need a well, how deep must it go and how much volume should it contain? Are there trees you'll want or need to take down, and if so, are there any special environmental regulations concerning that? Are there a lot of rocks and boulders—particularly hidden ones—that will need to be removed when building or adding a pool or deck?

Foundation: What kind of foundation does the site require and how expensive will it be? Is concrete readily available nearby or will it cost a lot to get it to the site?

Future construction: Will there be construction by any nearby lot owners or the city or local government? This could effect your view, privacy, or home value. What about traffic? Is there any near the future home? Will there be any roads built in the future? Aside from noise considerations, the carbon monoxide from traffic can severely interfere with growing gardens and developing landscapes.

Views: Plan for what you want each of your windows or curtain walls to overlook. If you know ahead of time which home you want, you might choose the land based on the views it allows. Or, if you love the land and want to live there, you can pick or design the house for the views.

Sun and light: Consider what direction your home will face on the site. With all the glass used in many of today's prefab homes, it is important to consider where the sun rises and sets in relation to the house. Does the sun shine on the front of the house in the mornings, afternoons, or both? What effect will the sunshine have on energy efficiency? If you're planning a pool or deck, how long, and at what times of the day, will the sun hit them? Will it be shining most brightly when they are being used?

Character of the site: Review the shape and style of your property. How will your choice of home fit there? Consider the distances from the back, side, and front yards and the property lines. Does it all make sense? Don't forget about allowing room for a deck, a pool, or just privacy.

Safety of the site: Is the land in a low-lying area or one that has a lot of trees? What is the potential for flooding or fires? Are fire, police, and other support close by? What is the response times for these services? These considerations can affect not only the vital matter of safety, but insurance costs as well—premiums can be huge if the services are not quality or aren't located within a reasonable distance.

contractors

Even with prefab, the likelihood is that you will need one or more contractors, though far less in number and for far less time than with conventional building. Even if it is just for one purpose, like connecting the electrical system, it is important to get information and references before hiring anyone.

Contractors in the area: Is your site close to a selection of contractors, or will they have to travel far to get to it? Are they available, or is there a long wait for them?

What to ask contractors: Get their track record on getting jobs done on time and on budget. Have they been willing to fix problems and misunderstandings that come up? Have they ever had fines levied by a state board or a court as a result of a complaint? Does their contract allow for both parties to put disputes in front of a licensed mediator before going to an attorney or pursing a lawsuit? Ask for three customers to use as references.

What to ask fellow customers: It may seem like a lot of work, but these are questions worth asking. It'll pay off in the end—saving you both money and stress—if you screen out a bad contractor and end up with a good one.

- How did the customer find the contractor?
- Did the project begin on the date agreed upon?
- Did the contractor show up on time each day?
- Did the customer get a detailed estimate before the contract?
- Did the customer get everything in writing, or did they have to ask for it? Did the contractor resist a written work statement?
- Was the job finished on time and with the quality promised? If not, why not, and did the contractor try to charge the customer more money for the extra time?
- Did the contractor complete the job within the cost estimate? Did the contractor talk to the customer about extra charges, and if so, were they justified?
- Was the customer able to contact the contractor easily? Was the customer given a cell phone or pager number?

- How was the work overall? Would the customer hire the contractor again?
- Were the contractor and crew professional and relatively friendly?

What to ask for from a contractor: Get a Request for quote (RFQ) for each type of contracting job you need done. Send everyone you want to consider using for the project an RFQ for competing bids. See that they are comfortable with the idea of working with prefab; some workers resist the notion.

saving money

You want the home you want and you should get it. But as the ability to custom design prefab grows, there are ways you can work with the architect to bring costs down if you are willing to consider a few different options.

Design the home to be cost-effective: A deck will cost less than a porch, because a porch requires both a floor and ceiling system. Open rooms are a trademark of many of today's prefab homes, but they don't allow supports for upstairs rooms, so make sure the rest of the house is planned carefully if there are one or more major open spaces.

Get the best costs on materials: Again, your architect may already have the best costs, but you can make sure that materials, tools, and supplies come from wholesale stores. Both prefab materials and conventional materials used for finishing are more readily available on the Internet than ever before, so search it for the best prices; you can save up to 20 percent this way.

Get tax breaks: If you plan on running any kind of business, no matter how part-time, with the intent of making a profit, you can write off up to 23 percent of your house. It doesn't matter if the house is prefab or mobile, as long as it is the house where you do that business, so consider this when deciding whether to include a study or office in the house.

You'll have a much easier time with a prefab house than with conventional building, but a house is a house and it's best to take on the endeavor seriously. Following these guidelines should help you do that without feeling over burdened.

sources

architects and designers

Alchemy
Geoffrey Warner and Paul Stankey
550 Vandalia Street, #314
St. Paul, MN 55114
651-647-6650
alchemyarchitecture.com

Anderson Anderson Architecture
Peter Anderson and Mark Anderson
83 Columbia Street, Suite 300
Seattle, WA 98104
2332 Fifth Street
Berkeley, CA 94710
206-332-9500 | 510-849-4380
(fax) 425-671-0050
andersonanderson.com

Anshen + Allen Architects
anshen.com

Michael Bell Architecture
155 West 60th Street, #1626
New York, NY 10023
212-721-2395
michael-bell.net

Edgar Blazona
2729 Acton Street
Berkeley, CA 94702
415-350-4904
modulardwellings.com
edgar@modulardwellings.com

BW|AR
Blake Williams, AIA
208 Koch Avenue
Anne Arbor, MI 48103
734-761-1670
blake_020965@hotmail.com

Central Office of Architecture
323-936-9210
coalabs.com
info@coalabs.com

Choi-Campagna Design
choicampagna@aol.com

Collins and Turner
Penelope Collins and Huw Turner
Studio 3, 151 Foveaux Street
Surry Hills, NSW 2010 Australia
612-9356-3217
mail@collinsandturner.com

Piercy Connor
Cairo Studios
4–6 Nile Street
London N1 7RF England
020-7490-9494
piercyconner.co.uk
info@tdrinc.com

etekt.com
Cutting-edge source for architects and their house designs.

First Penthouse
firstpenthouse.co.uk

Michael Graves & Associates
341 Nassau Street
Princeton, NJ 08540
609-924-6409
(fax) 609-924-1795
michaelgraves.com

Heikkinen-Komonen Architects
Kristianinkatu 11–13
00170 Helsinki Finland
358-9-75102111
heikkinen-komonen.fi
ak@heikkinen-komonen.fi

David Hertz
2908 Colorado Avenue
Santa Monica, CA 90404
310-829-9932
(fax) 310-829-5641
syndesisinc.com
hertzaia@syndesisinc.com

Steven Holl
450 West 31st Street
New York, NY 10001
212-629-7262
(fax) 212-629-7312
stevenholl.com
mail@stevenholl.com

Jones, Partners: Architecture
Wes Jones
141 Nevada Street
El Segundo, CA 90245
310-414-0761
jonespartners.com
info@jonespartners.com

Kalkin & Company
Adam Kalkin
59-65 Mine Brook Road
Bernardsville, NJ 07924
908-696-1999
(fax) 908-696-1998
architectureandhygiene.com

KFN
Oskar Leo Kaufmann
Steinebach 3
6850 Dornbirn Austria
43-5572-394969
olk.cc
office@olk.cc

KOL/MAC Studio
Sultan Kolatan
kolatanmacdonaldstudio.com

KRDB
Christopher Robertson and Chris Krager
5210 Avenue F
Austin, TX 78751
512-374-0946
lividpencil.com
krdb@lividpencil.com

Lewis.Tsurumaki.Lewis
147 Essex Street
New York, NY 10002
212-505-5955
office@LTLwork.net

LOT-EK
info@lot-ek.com

LuxeBox
luxeboxliving.com
info@luxeboxliving.com

Marmol Radziner and Associates
Leo Marmol
12210 Nebraska Avenue
Los Angeles, CA 90025
310-826-6222
marmol-radziner.com
mail@marmol-radziner.com

William Massie Architecture
274 2nd Street
Troy, NY 12180
518-274-0303
massiearchitecture.com
info@massiearchitecture.com

M-House
Tim Pyne
The Workhouse
31 Charlotte Road
London EC2A 3PB England
020-7739-3367
m-house.org

mk Architecture
Michelle Kaufmann
mkarchitecture.com
michelle@mkarchitecture.com

Modern Modular
www.modern-modular.com

Nottoscale
Matthias Troitzsch and Peter Strzebniok
130 Sutter Street, Suite 300
San Francisco, CA 94110
415-433-0120, ext. 263, 296
nottoscale.com
info@nottoscale.com

pH Architects
David Pysh, Alex Hurst
pharchitects.com

Randolph Designs
John Randolph
601 Minnesota Street, Studio 216
San Francisco, CA 94107-3055
415-821-9881
randolphdesigns.com
john@randolphdesigns.com

Reilly + Grice Design
3126 West Cary Street, #430
Richmond, VA 23221
804-502-9590
reillygrice.com
alastair@reillygrice.com

Resolution: 4 Architecture
Joseph Tanney and Robert Luntz
150 West 28th Street, Suite 1902
New York, NY 10001
212-675-9266
(fax) 212-206-0944
re4a.com
jtanney@re4a.com

Rocio Romero
rocioromero.com
contact@rocioromero.com

Shelter-Kit Incorporated
22W Mill Street
Tilton, NH 03276
shelter-kit.com

Siegal Office of Mobile Design
Jennifer Siegal
1725 Abbot Kinney Boulevard
Venice, CA 90291
310-439-1129
(fax) 310-439-2495
designmobile.com

Philippe Starck
18/20 Rue du Faubourg du Temple
75011 Paris France
330-1-48-07-5454
philippe-starck.com
info@philippe-starck.com

su11 Architecture + Design
Erich Schoenenberger and Ferda Kolatan
9 Debrosses Street, Suite 515
New York, NY 10013
212-941-6494
(fax) 212-941-6496
su11.com
sberger@su11.com

Tsui Design and Research
Eugene Tsui
6 Admiral Drive, Suite 272
Emeryville, CA 94608
510-658-8989
tdrinc.com
info@tdrinc.com

White on White
212-964-4694

Richard Wintersole
649 Quail Ridge
Aledo, TX 76008
817-441-9783
margrick@hcnews.com

materials

americanbamboo.org

A. Zahner Architectural Metals
1400 E. 9th Street
Kansas City, MO 84106
816-474-8882
azahner.com

Alusion
6320-2 Danville Road
Mississauga, Ontario
Canada L5T 2L7
905-696-9300
alusion.com
info@alusion.com

Atco Structures
800-575-2826
atcostructures.com
"Rapid Roof" system for containers.

Butler Manufacturing
cewills@butlermfg.org

Classic Steel Frame Homes
7313 Fairview
Houston, TX 77041
800-624-4663 | 713-896-7425
(fax) 713-896-8909
metalhomes.com
sales-marketing@metalhomes.com

Government Liquidation
govliquidation.com
Surplus U.S. government containers for sale.

isocontainers.com
876 Land Street
East Riverton, NJ 08077
856-303-1101

Martin Container Inc.
1402 East Lomita Boulevard
Wilmington, CA 90748
800-221-3727
container.com

Nana Wall Systems
nanawallsystems.com

P&O Nedlloyd
ponl.com

plybooamerica.com

Sea Box, Inc.
802 Industrial Highway
East Riverton, NJ 08077
499 Hollywood Ave.
South Plainfield, NJ 07080
856-303-1101
(fax) 856-303-1501
sales@seabox.com

Syndesis
2908 Colorado Avenue
Santa Monica, CA 90404
310-829-9932
(fax) 310-829-5641
syndesisinc.com

Tandemloc Inc.
824 Highway 101
Havelock, NC 28532
800-258-7324
(fax) 800-892-3273
tandemloc.com
Fittings, hardware, and connectors for containers.

Transport Information Service
tis-gdv.com
General information on containers.

stores and manufacturers

David Schreyr
609-933-5813
d.shreyr@verizon.net

Design Within Reach
800-944-2233
(fax) 800-846-0411
designwithinreach.com
Modern furniture and lighting.

European Furniture Importers
800-243-1955
EuroFurniture.com
Modern furnishings and accessories.

Ikea
boklok.com

Lindal Cedar Homes
lindal.com

Royal Homes
Royal Homes Toronto Studio
3 Bridgman Avenue, #202
Toronto, Ontario M5R 2V4 Canada
royalhomestoronto.com
lloyd@royalhomes.com

Target
target.com

information and organizations

Architecture for Humanity
Cameron Sinclair, Founder
646-765-0906
csinclair@architectureforhumanity.org
Solutions for transitional housing for people in crisis around the world.

ArchitectureWeek.com

archleague.org

Chicago Landmarks
CityofChicago.org

Design Architecture
designarchitecture.com

ezlogkits.com
For general information on panelized homes.

fabprefab.com

Gabion
hughpearman.com
Writing on architecture and design.

galinsky.com
On modern buildings.

imodular.com

jetsetmodern.com

The Key Center for Architectural Sociology
archsoc.com
Research and findings on architecture
and society.

Modern Sustainable Living
mome.org
Explores modern housing for a larger market.

Modular Building Institute
413 Park Street
Charlottesville, VA 22902
888-811-3288 | 434-296-3288
(fax) 434-296-3361
info@mbinet.org

National Association of Home Builders
1201 15th Street, NW
Washington, DC 20005
Building Systems Councils Hotline
800-368-5242
buildingsystems.org
Write or call for a free brochure on
prefab housing.

Prefabs.co.uk

credits

Nicholas Kane, p. 1. 82, 85, 87
Studio Markku Alatalo, Helsinki, p. 2–3, 42, 45, 46, 47, 48, 49
Peter Aaron/Esto, p. 6–7, 50, 52, 53, 54, 55
Daniel Hennessy, p. 8–9, 66, 69, 70, 71, 72, 73
Tim Street-Porter/Esto, p.5, 26,
Courtesy Richard Wintersole, p.10, 34, 35, 36, 37, 38, 39, 40,
    41, 148
Courtesy Athenaeum of Philadelphia, p. 14, 15
Courtesy Estate of R. Buckminster Fuller, p. 16
From the Collections of The Henry Ford, p. 17
Courtesy Hans-Josef Kuepper, p. 18
Library of Congress, Prints and Photographs Division, Historic American
    Buildings Survey, Historic American Engineering Record, p. 21
Ezra Stoller/Esto, p. 22
Jack Boucher. Library of Congress, Prints and Photographs Division,
    Historic American Buildings Survey, Historic American Engineering
    Record, p. 23, 25
Julius Shulman, p. 28, 29
Courtesy Richard J. L. Martin, President, Global Peace Containers,
    a subsidiary of New Generation Partnerships, p. 30
Alex Bartel/Esto, p. 31
Courtesy Shelburne Museum, Vermont, p. 56, 57
Courtesy Adam Kalkin, p. 58, 59
Julio Pereira, Courtesy Rocio Romero, p. 60, 62, 63, 149

Courtesy Rocio Romero, p. 64, 65
Courtesy Jennifer Siegal/Office of Mobile Design, p. 74, 75, 147
Courtesy Tim Pyne, p. 76, 78, 79, 80, 81
Ignacio Martinez, p. 89, 90, 91, 94, 95, 96, 97
Courtesy Oskar Leo Kaufmann, p. 92–93 (above)
Adolf Bereuter, p. 92–93 (below)
Courtesy GA Photographers, p. 99, 100
Courtesy Colllins and Turner, p. 103, 104–105, 106, 108
Karen Moskowitz, p. 110, 113, 114,
Courtesy Steven Holl, p. 117
Courtesy Resolution: 4 Architecture, p. 119, 121, 122, 125
Courtesy Michael Graves & Associates, p. 127, 128
Courtesy su11 Architecture + Design, p. 131, 132, 151
Star Tribune, Minneapolis, p. 136
Courtesy Edgar Blazona, p. 137 (above)
Courtesy Choi-Campagna Design, p. 137 (below)
Courtesy Jones, Partners: Architecture, p. 138 (below)
Courtesy Lewis.Tsurumaki.Lewis, p. 138 (above)
Courtesy of Paul Warchol, p. 139 (above)
MBR Studios, Courtesy mkarchitecture, p. 140
Courtesy Nottoscale, p. 141 (above)
Courtesy pH Architects, p. 142 (below)
Courtesy White on White Design, p. 142 (below)
Courtesy Blake Williams, p. 143

index